PENCILS AND PURPOSE

PENCILS AND PURPOSE

How Twelve Visionaries Sketched a New Blueprint for Education

RAKESH GUPTA | UDAYAN NATH | SUMIT HANDA

HARPER LEARNING

An Imprint of HarperCollins *Publishers*
www.harpercollins.co.in

First published in India by Harper Learning 2026
An imprint of HarperCollins *Publishers*
HarperCollins Publishers India, Cyber City,
Building 10-A, Gurugram, Haryana – 122002, India
www.harpercollins.co.in

2 4 6 8 10 9 7 5 3 1

P-ISBN: 978-93-7307-949-3
E-ISBN: 978-93-7307-766-6

Typeset in 11.5 pt/15 Adobe Garamond Pro
by HarperCollins *Publishers* India Pvt. Ltd

Printed and bound at
Manipal Technologies Limited, Manipal

MIX
Paper | Supporting responsible forestry
FSC www.fsc.org FSC™ C043100

This book is produced from independently certified FSC® paper to ensure responsible forest management.

*

HarperCollins *Publishers*, Macken House, 39/40 Mayor Street Upper, Dublin 1, D01 C9W8, Ireland

To the community working every day to improve education

Contents

Section 3: Changing Systems

Author's Note

Every great change in education begins with something small—a line drawn by a pencil; a thought written in the quiet of belief. That small pencil, sharpened by knowledge, holds the promise of beginnings. It is simple, unassuming, yet capable of shaping worlds. In its fragile lead lies the power to question, to create, and to rewrite the stories of generations.

Purpose is what gives that power direction. It turns a simple mark on paper into a movement of minds. It pushes people to become extraordinary. Purpose is what takes the evolving idea and carries it through failure, resistance, and time until it becomes a lasting light for others.

The twelve education entrepreneurs in this book began with ideas as delicate as pencil strokes and turned them into institutions that continue to define how the world learns. Each one shows that education is not only about knowledge but about intent, seeing the unseen potential in people, and believing that change can be drawn into being.

This book, *Pencils and Purpose*, is a celebration of those who never stopped writing the story of hope through education. It reminds us of what begins as a single line on a blank page can become a map for millions to find their way toward a better tomorrow.

Introduction

The Windows and Mirrors of Education

Let us start with some striking data which captures this telling narrative. Over the last 200 years, literacy rates in the world as we know it has seen a dramatic shift. If less than 20 per cent of the world was literate in the 1800s; today, less than 20 per cent is illiterate at a global level.

That might seem like a remarkable achievement when one sees the world from the context of a few hundred years instead of a few years or even a few decades. But the bigger truth is that a country's education level is deeply connected to other social and economic outcomes.

In India, since ancient times, we had gurukuls imparting holistic and other traditional forms of tuition before there was a mass scale formalization of education. Education, especially when connected to work and career can sustain one's family, has evolved slowly over time with multiple streams of possibilities. Beyond formal college education, which is still relatively a recent phenomenon; the focus on learning a trade to master that craft was more in vogue earlier.

Let us recall a point in time when things pivoted to understand this better.

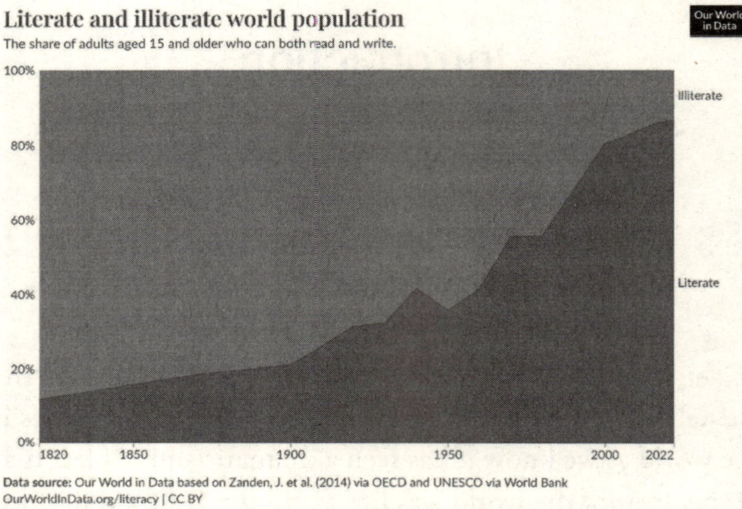

The period we are speaking of is the fourteenth and fifteenth century. The setting was Italy, particularly the picturesque city of Florence. Today, as we travel around the place and gaze, awe-inspired, at the majestic church paintings, the stone sculptures and the majestic art in this beautiful city, we remember the brilliant artists and sculptors who gave rise to these timeless artefacts of creativity. Some might go a step further, and remember the benefactors of the art, who gave them these commissions and supported the artists as they toiled away at their masterpieces.

But, beneath all of that, there was another phenomenon at work which helped these creations to come to life. In the late fifteenth century, there were allegedly fifty-four workshops for working on marble and stone artefacts, which employed painters and many master gold and silversmiths. It is said, given the premium art and patronage from wealthy families, the city had more woodcarvers than butchers!

Leonardo Da Vinci, considered to be one of the most celebrated polymaths today, started off as one such apprentice artist, at the age of fourteen. It was recorded that he learnt the skills from the celebrated expert Verrocchio, helping the Master with the paintings before working independently on commissioned pieces.

In fact, in an interesting explanation, an article from *Star Tribune* explained that the word "masterpiece"—a word we use to attribute exceptional works of creativity even today, originated during this period when apprentices had to showcase their skills to the guild, a body which governed craftworks including metalwork, enamelling, etc. It was a rite of passage which, if demonstrated successfully, would allow the apprentice to become a master in their own turn and be authorized to train others. Different guilds specified different rules for the road from apprenticeship to mastery.

In India, the earlier established model of education from gurukuls to gharanas for music exemplified this kind of immersive and skill-based training that prepared people for a lifetime. Imagine a young musician training at the music maestro or Ustaad's house with years of rigorous practice before becoming a qualified musician.

Extrapolating this from the world of arts and creativity, the book called *Mastery* by Robert Greene brought to light multiple examples across different walks of life that exemplified the same approach of apprenticeship to mastery in a specific area of skill.

As a part of this approach, the intriguing story of Michael Faraday and Humphry Davy stands out. Born to a poor family in the late 1700s, Faraday had little scope for formal education, which was limited at that time, to a select few and privileged sect of society. But he found an opportunity to apprentice in a bookbinding shop and read many books during his time there. Among these books, he read about electricity, an exciting new area of scientific innovation that was taking its early strides during this time. Not just that, he also heard the discussions of the scientist Sir Humphry Davy. He wanted to work with Davy, but he had no direct access to him. Putting his bookbinding skills to good use, he made a beautiful binding of his detailed notes and presented it to him. Later, he not only started working with Davy, but became more celebrated than his mentor in the world of science for his contributions to the laws of electrolysis. This is both a story of grit and the power of the apprenticeship training model on the road to true skills mastery.

History is littered with similar stories and examples that shine the light on a few key characteristics which links education and profession.

First, among examples of informal learning, is the power of self-learning, similar to Faraday's approach of building his own skills. Today, it is much easier to self-learn with myriads of free tools available online. However, it can be intimidating to navigate the overwhelming breadth of information available and to navigate between truth and misinformation.

Second, is the apprenticeship method of honing one's skills for years under tutelage before becoming a master. This provides the kind of in-depth and practical training which transfers well in the professional world along with one's formal education instead of only holding a certificate.

These learnings are especially prominent in today's changing times when the link between education and jobs is getting challenged by the rapid shifts in technology and its impact on work. But before we get to the predicted future, let us examine the emergence of structured or 'formal' education, a system which brought structure and consistency through the methods of a planned syllabi and learning assessments.

While self-learning and skill-based learning have immense advantages, in the ages before formal education—schools, colleges and universities—education was restricted to the privileged class. Access to knowledge was a display of power and was often used to discriminate against people.

Barring that access to high quality knowledge, many people had to apprentice under their family members and acquire basic practical skills over technical know-hows and expansion of expertise. In cases these skills or crafts were not highly valued by the market, the families were unable to move out of their class structure and struggled to escape abject poverty over generations. There was also an element of caste-based discrimination, especially in India through this, as certain groups were only assumed to be 'fit' for certain work. The book *Hunger Games* by Suzanne Collins showcased this powerfully as the world-building exhibited skill-based formation of districts—division of industries and labour based on the type of service (mining, agriculture, fishing, etc.)—which decided the economical strata and Capitol's investment during the brutal games.

Formal education, as it developed, was meant to be an equalizer for people, broad basing the access to education for everyone, regardless of their status in society's hierarchy. It was therefore a chance to take a step beyond the family background and occupations to craft new dreams, based on one's ability to grasp new skills and sheer determination. Even today, there is a lifetime value of networks and skills one gets upon acing tough examinations and attending premier institutions with hard work and intelligence. These opportunities elevate an individual and provides them and their loved ones with sustained income.

No wonder that in a country such as India, which is home to one of the largest groups of young people globally, these competitive examinations—be it for engineering pursuits, medical professions or government jobs—are immensely difficult to qualify for. Multiple books and movies show the hard path students need to take to prepare for these examinations to emerge victorious among lakhs of other candidates. What can we do to make higher education more accessible to students without them having to jump through hoops to achieve their dreams?

Over the last few decades, with a slew of initiatives, our country has been successful in increasing enrolment of children in school coming from all backgrounds. Our primary school enrolment rates have consistently increased. However, as children progress through levels of education, there are still a high number of students dropping their education mid-way.

By the time college education starts, we have an estimate of 28 per cent enrolment rates for formal education. That still leaves two challenges which are intrinsically linked to the world of work.

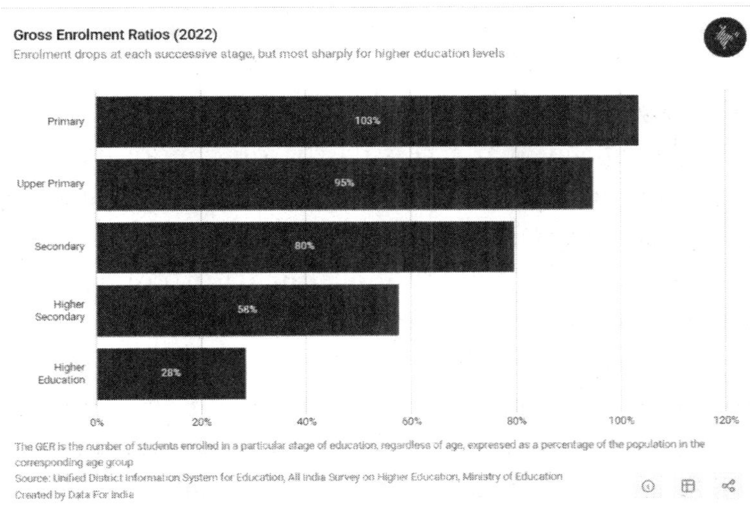

First and foremost is the quality of education. Foundational literacy and numeracy skills (FLN), as defined by World Bank, is the ability to read simple text or perform simple addition and subtraction Despite more primary level students, the quality of foundation is still far from being adequate at grade level. In fact, World Bank's Learning Poverty Indicator recommends that by age ten, or by grade two, children should be able to read simple text else it leads to a learning poverty.

The number for learning poverty for India, pre-pandemic, was at a 50 per cent. During the pandemic, schools closed globally for prolonged periods of time. This, in turn, led to a further drop in foundational learning levels for children. Specially those without digital access to education found themselves at a significant disadvantage. Disruptions from external events—natural disasters, pandemics or wars—have historically caused issues with learning as well.

As the educational access has become more uniform over time, the gaps in learning are showing up starkly as educational quality issues. According to multiple education experts and early childhood education companies, foundational learning and the accompanied knowledge of language is a leading indicator for learning levels. Whether it is solving word problems in math or understanding scientific and social concepts, language remains a key denominator in the indication of a child's grasp on understanding a subject. If children fall behind on this, it is tough for them after the age of ten to improve on their foundational skills.

One can blame the very linear and competitive nature of the education system today. For some people, the approach to formal education, defined as the Macaulay model of education created by the British in India, was a flawed one as the basic objective was to train people in skills required to support the East India Company's ambitions. It did not seek to encourage independent thinking.

Many great Indian social reformists from Tagore to Raja Ram Mohan Roy to Vidyasagar have spoken about the true nature of education—the ability to think critically and make decisions for the betterment of society. While we have built globally renowned institutions of learning today, the demand of education and work opportunities continues to be irreversibly proportional to the supply of its provision. To look at the numbers in context, we have over 500 million people, with access to education, skills to income and to job portals, in the ages between eighteen and forty.

The New Education Policy 2020 has been one key step in the right direction; bringing changes in Board Examination patterns, advocating for a single college entrance examination, deeper focus on improving quality of foundational learning, and enabling skill based Higher Education.

Given that higher education enrolment in India is less than 30 per cent, one immediate and short-term solution to enhance educational outcomes is to increase that ratio and to have more young people attend college. But the link between education and jobs is not so simple.

Given the changing nature of jobs and technology, there have been more questions about possible educated unemployment. Additionally, the cost of college degrees, which in many cases, brings the burden of student debt. Another trend noticeable is the preference for foreign college education. With the new Education guidelines and the collaborations with international universities, it is hoped that the choice for Indian students is going to increase. The New

Education Policy has also laid the groundwork for a flexible credit system where students can have multiple entry and exit points from the academic system, combining courses from colleges with high quality online certificate programs based. All these initiatives, individually or taken together, could address the gross enrolment ratio and encourage more people to pursue college. It can also help reduce the financial burden on students. In different ways, it could open different financial pathways for attending colleges with a hybrid model as it widens accessibility beyond physical proximity.

But increasing higher education enrolment is futile without focusing on the employability turnover. A major challenge witnessed by our country is low employability options, from campus career portals and external sources, especially at 'fresher' levels. What is clear is that degrees alone may not be enough.

Not just that, with generative AI making rapid advances in more high-end work, the possible redundancy of humans being hired is getting questioned. While there are wild guesses and doomsday estimates, cautious experts say that Gen AI will be more of a collaborator than a displacer of jobs, but the other pertinent area would be to focus on upskilling workforce in areas of high-demand jobs, which may not be purely white collar in terms of nature. Would the world not need more drone operators as drones start to be used in industries varying from agriculture to ecommerce? What about mobile phone repair jobs as everyone owns a mobile? Such skill-based jobs and even micro-entrepreneurship opportunities will need the right incentives and dignity to be recognized and to be made aspirational for people.

This is urgent as the outcome for many people who are currently in the education system is the promise of stable income. Which in many cases means jobs where we see the biggest gaps across sectors today.

This book shines the light on people who have spent their lives trying to bring much needed change across the entire value chain of the education system.

The central argument in this book, the link between education and jobs, brings this question to focus more clearly than ever: Can we, as a nation, create enough jobs for the hundreds of millions of young people in our country?

What will be the biggest motivators for work?

There are already some tectonic changes. IT Services, which had traditionally provided several jobs for engineers and consequently built the engineering demand has reduced their hiring levels with the onset of newer technologies. On the other hand, e-commerce or 'quick' commerce industries are expected to grow exponentially, bringing in a demand for skilled workers in logistics, supply and distribution. But are they providing the right career progression, regulatory support and long-term growth for people? What percentage of that will constitute the overall workforce in the next century? This will be a key question to assess.

Some people believe that climate action facing jobs will increase. It will, again, have nuances. There could be jobs that focus on innovation in sustainability and climate action.

There will be other jobs that will help shift existing companies towards more climate friendly practices. Finally, every job could have a climate or sustainability component over time, regardless of the sector or the function.

Semiconductors are one emerging area of investment and support.

Meanwhile other emerging sectors, be it energy efficient vehicles or cybersecurity, will also evolve. Through all these emerging shifts, the evergreen jobs like educators, medical professionals, lawyers and such will continue to be in-demand. Can one even imagine a world without these qualified professionals?

As Morgan Housel shared in his brilliant book, *Psychology of Money*, and in his subsequent book, *Same as Ever*, there are temporary and permanent shifts in the world around us. The temporary shifts seem to be massive when they occur, but they do not change the underlying behaviour. For example, with the onset of the COVID pandemic many thought that learning online would be the way forward. As time showed, children needed schools. For learning, yes. But for much more too. The structured environment of the school, the platonic relationships built, the physical education and more shape their young minds. It is also the place of trust for the parents when it comes to education. While online learning can supplement and add to that, especially for younger kids, schools were not going to ever become irrelevant. It is a classic example of one such temporary shift which some people overestimated and believed to be a permanent shift. Some even made wrong investments with this assumption.

In the world of jobs around us today, there are many more such emerging temporary and permanent shifts. What is critical is for each one of us, individually and collectively, to assess these shifts and plan our actions accordingly.

'*Learning How To Learn*' is one of the most learnt courses at Global Edtech firm, Coursera. Talentsprint, another global Edtech firm, brings in the capacity of learning how to learn by introducing '*Learning With Peers*' and '*Learning With Failure*' as key elements of their pedagogy.

The other interconnected aspect is the need to dispel the myth of a linear learning path. We can no longer afford to learn for a few years, get a degree, work for a certain number of years and then retire. People have the freedom of choice to navigate between education and profession at any point in their life. They can opt for working right after graduation instead of pursuing higher studies and come back to it years later; they can opt for pursuing education till they're old and sustain themselves with part time jobs and starting small businesses. The linear path of education to career, as taught by our previous generations, no longer holds true. 'Lifelong learning' as it is famously called today could extend our learning far beyond formal education years. It introduces a chance to develop and use new skills, explore new careers at different points of life

Again, this is not a new model. Back in the Renaissance period, which gave us some of the best music and art, the concept of a polymath was well appreciated. People specialized, not just in one area, but had interests in different areas and through that unique combination of interests, were able to find new meanings in old problems.

Da Vinci was a classic example of someone who was not just a painter and a sculptor but also an engineer, a designer of multiple practical artefacts, product engineer, and more.

With more uncertainty around us, the established linear route of education followed by a singular speciality job before eventually retirement could be a pattern that is tending beyond its expiry date. In simpler terms, a permanent shift might be needed in terms of how we think of the interconnections between education and work at multiple points of time. The best careers of the emerging century could be ones where we do not sign up for one career for life, but give ourselves time to learn, to meander and to keep agility and learnability as the core of our approach to work.

Meet the Changemakers

Considering that education is the cornerstone of a nation's progress, the true transformation must begin at the grassroots, starting with reforms in K-12, extending to higher education and continuing into corporate upskilling. However, this is not solely the government's responsibility. Industry leaders, philanthropists, or anyone with the potential to initiate change must contribute meaningfully to transforming the Indian education sector.

From Savitribai Phule, who opened India's first girls school in 1848, to Dr B.R Ambedkar, who promoted social empowerment; Rabindranath Tagore, champion of experiential learning; Jamsetji Tata, the visionary behind the Indian Institute of Science; and Annie Besant, an educationist who strongly believed in education for nation building, the pages of history are filled with individuals who helped shape India by leveraging the power of education.

Every decade has seen reformers who have used education and their privilege to uplift the masses and make education more accessible to everyone. This book has attempted to capture the inspiring work of such individuals who, through their own educational awakenings in recent years, discovered the gaps in the Indian education sector and paved the way for future generations to embrace the dynamics of modern education as a fundamental necessity of life.

Shaheen Mistri, Founder of 'Teach for India'

To begin with, is the incredible story of Shaheen Mistri, the founder of Teach for India, a renowned name in the educational and social impact circles. A woman, well-aware of her own privileges, reflects on her own global experiences and decides to get back to her roots to address the issue of education inequity in India. What began as a vision to educate and offer the necessities of life to the underprivileged children through the Akanksha Foundation—an after-school initiative—soon turned into a national movement.

At the time, little did she know that Akanksha Foundation would inspire her to lay the bricks for Teach for India, in-turn creating a ripple effect and envisioning a nation-wide presence.

From a very young age, Mistri became aware of the privileges she had—privileges many others around her did not. Mistri clearly saw the stark difference between the way the world treated the underprivileged, and how education, too, was often reserved for the elite. This awareness gradually turned into determination to break through existing social mindsets that hindered equal access to education.

Hers is a story of realisation, resilience, and impact—one that continues to empower young minds towards building rewarding futures and rewriting family histories.

Kiranbir Sethi, Founder of Riverside School and Design For Change

Another name that has revolutionized K-12 education through strategic designing is Kiranbir Sethi, the founder of Riverside School. What began as a mother's concern about fear-driven discipline against her son evolved into a strong urge to completely transform the existing system.

While her own childhood, under the shelter of progressive parents, allowed her the freedom to explore her desires, she knew not everyone's life offered the same opportunity. Hence, she decided to design a school that would become a place where children could grow and graduate as aware and conscious citizens of the country.

In contrast to the traditional schooling that she acquired, it was her decision to enrol at NID (National Institute of Design) that completely changed her view of education and how it should be imparted. It was there that she got introduced to the power of 'what if'—a feeling that pushes an individual to go beyond the set norms and delve deep into the sea of creativity; and ask oneself how it would feel to actually travel down the road not yet taken.

It was this belief that everything should be designed by keeping in mind the requirements of the end user that eventually became the blueprint for the Riverside school. With her team, she developed the 'FIDS' framework—Feel, Imagine, Do, and Share—which was incorporated in almost everything, from designing curriculum to developing policies for employee retention, to turn every individual that they crossed paths with into strategic changemakers.

It is through clarity and unwavering determination that she decided to take her vision beyond classrooms. As a result, she launched aProCh initiative to make cities more children-friendly, and Design for Change (DFC) that offered self-explanatory toolkits for schools across India and abroad, to include the concept of design for change in their curriculum. Today, DFC is not only dedicated to solving challenges across the globe but also empowers students to grow into citizens with a vision and voice.

Dr J C Chaudhry, Founder of Aakash Institute

Aakash Institute, a name synonymous with excellent test preparation in India, started as a small coaching centre in Delhi with a mere investment of Rs 2,000 by a revolutionary visionary—*Dr J C Chaudhry.* Born and brought up in a humble environment, the values of simplicity and discipline played a pivotal role in keeping him focussed on the idea of offering quality education to students.

In addition, his own encounters with some incredible teachers shaped his own principles that later became the foundational pillars of the Aakash Institute. During his formative years, one of the teachers taught him the importance of strengthening the fundamentals before advancing to complex themes, and this became his core teaching philosophy—one he swears by to this day.

Even as the competition in the coaching sector intensified, with multiple institutes spending in premium ad services to attract young minds, Chaudhry valued credibility over visibility. His success was a result of his commitment to quality education and not a humongous advertisement campaign. Not only JC, his son Aakash, also eventually brought his own potential to the table and propelled the institute into a new era of growth by embracing digitalization as a natural progression.

That said, JC is a man of many talents. Along with playing the role of a profound educator, his passion for numerology allowed him to enter a new entrepreneurial venture and supported the success of the institute and his family members. He firmly believes that numbers carry vibrations that can unlock powerful transformations. He has used numerology to help many individuals he crossed paths with to discover their true potential.

His mission has not only been to nurture the talents of the youth, but also to serve humanity in every way possible by leveraging his brand 'Aakash.' Today, this name not only stands as a testament to JC's excellence in the education sector but also in the healthcare area, where his son continues to carry his legacy and unparalleled commitment to the greater good of the society. His story is a stark reminder of one's purpose doesn't cease to exist; it continues to evolve and take on new forms.

Grace Pinto and Family, Founder of Ryan International Schools

Ryan International is a name that needs no introduction in India—an institution known for offering premium quality education and most importantly, for imparting value-based education. Grace Pinto, after her marriage to Dr Augustine F Pinto, drew inspiration from Mother Teresa's journey and decided to open an institution that could nurture young talent in ways existing schools failed to. Along with academic knowledge, the school promised intellectual and behavioural values, blending moral and spiritual belief systems to ensure every 'Ryanite' builds a rewarding and righteous career path.

For Grace, serving as a Managing Director meant going beyond the walls of her office to interact with parents and teachers, understand their concerns and come up with the best possible solutions. Their goal was never just expansion just in terms of branches, but in terms of meaningful impact.

Along with addressing the growth needs of the students, Grace has always been deeply committed to the growth of all her teachers as well. She personally oversees the hiring process and ensures their individual upskilling and training so that both the school and the teachers experience uninterrupted growth. While the school has received several accolades and recognitions, it is the stories of its alumni that stand testament to the hard work and unwavering dedication of the Pintos. Now entering its fifth decade, Ryan as an institution continues to expand its horizon, spreading its purpose-driven education across the globe.

Pramath Raj Sinha, Founder of Ashoka University and Harappa

From Patna to Penn and McKinsey to Ashoka, Pramath Raj Sinha's journey is a clear example of how those dedicated to empowering others don't wait for change—they initiate it. His desire to open a university that championed liberal arts education stemmed from his own experiences at IIT Kanpur and University of Pennsylvania.

While doing his master's and PhD in Engineering from Penn, he understood how global universities encouraged students to dive into different subjects each semester to understand their interests. Alongside earning his degrees in engineering, he chose to study the subjects of computer science and robotics, embracing an interdisciplinary approach.

When it comes to his professional refinement, Sinha gives complete credit to his years at McKinsey. His commitment to people, leadership abilities and business values are a result of the exposure and experience he got there—values that played a pivotal role in laying the foundation of Ashoka University and Harappa.

After redefining the business management education in India by becoming the founding dean of ISB, Sinha was sure that he wanted to offer an unmatched learning experience at Ashoka. His vision was to create a curriculum that allowed students to explore their interests across science, humanities and impact.

After launching Ashoka and running it successfully for years with like-minded leaders on a rotational leadership model, Sinha knew that skill development went beyond the classroom. Acknowledging the global demand for continuous upskilling in modern workplaces, he went on to launch Harappa, a digital skill enhancement platform, which was later acquired by upGrad. That said, every venture Sinha stepped into reflects his commitment to addressing the problems he witnessed in the education landscape while growing up and serves as his way of giving back to the society.

Ashish Dhawan, Founder of ChrysCapital, Central Square Foundation, Ashoka University, and The Convergence Foundation

A private equity titan turned philanthropist; Ashish Dhawan is widely regarded as one of the most influential changemakers in Indian education. After a successful career in finance, he stepped away from ChrysCapital to dedicate himself full-time to nation building. Through the Central Square Foundation, he has funded and supported hundreds of grassroots organizations that tackle systemic issues in school education. His role in co-founding Ashoka

University helped bring liberal arts education to the forefront of India's higher education narrative, while his Convergence Foundation aims to build catalytic institutions addressing India's toughest developmental challenges. Dhawan's work embodies the philosophy that true reform must come from a combination of philanthropic capital, visionary institutions, and collaborative governance. His story is one of reinvention, where personal success became the foundation for national service.

Ashwin Damera, Co-Founder of Eruditus and Emeritus

From chartered accountant to global edtech pioneer, Ashwin Damera represents the spirit of Indian entrepreneurship on a global stage. After an early corporate career and a pursued education at Harvard Business School, he ventured into a travel startup before finding his true calling in education. With Eruditus and its global brand Emeritus, he reimagined executive education by collaborating with the world's top universities, including Harvard, Wharton, INSEAD, and MIT, to make their programs accessible to professionals worldwide. His bold bet on affordability, blended learning, and international partnerships paid off, positioning Emeritus as one of India's first truly global edtech companies. Ashwin's journey is a testament to resilience, adaptability, and the conviction that education can be borderless.

Ronnie Screwvala, Founder of UTV and upGrad

A storyteller turned serial entrepreneur, Ronnie Screwvala has been a pioneer across industries, from media and entertainment to skill development and education. After revolutionizing India's film and television space with UTV, he turned his gaze to lifelong education with upGrad, one of India's most prominent edtech platforms. Ronnie's philosophy has always been rooted in scale and access, bringing high-quality opportunities to millions. He also set up Swades Foundation, focusing on rural empowerment. What makes him stand apart is his knack for anticipating change, whether in entertainment consumption in the '90s or digital learning in the 2010s. His journey highlights that true entrepreneurship is not about one successful venture but the ability to consistently reinvent oneself and create lasting impact.

Sunny Varkey, Founder of GEMS Education

Few names embody the globalization of education as strongly as Sunny Varkey. From a single Dubai school run by his parents in the 1960s, he built GEMS Education, the world's largest private K-12 school operator today, with a footprint across multiple continents. A visionary with a deep sense of purpose, Varkey believes in combining quality education with affordability and scale. Beyond his corporate empire, the Varkey Foundation focuses on teacher development and global education reform, famously instituting the Global Teacher Prize—a million-dollar award celebrating outstanding educators worldwide. For Varkey, education is both business and mission: a way to elevate societies, empower communities, and leave behind a legacy of enlightened generations.

Anita Karwal (Ex-IAS Officer and CBSE / NEP Leader)

A lifelong civil servant turned education reformer; Anita Karwal has been a key figure in shaping India's contemporary school education framework. As Chairperson of CBSE, she oversaw critical transitions including curriculum reforms and examination restructuring. Later, as Secretary of the Department of School Education and Literacy, she played a pivotal role in the rollout of the National Education Policy 2020, India's first major education policy reform in over three decades. Known for her empathetic yet decisive leadership, Karwal has consistently championed student well-being alongside academic rigor. Her work underscores the importance of governance, vision, and accountability in transforming education at scale.

Rajendra Pawar, Founder of NIIT

From engineering to entrepreneurship, the story of Rajendra Pawar, the founder of NIIT and famously recognized as the father of the IT sector in India, is a stark reminder of how one man's vision can script the growth journey of an entire nation beautifully.

Nurtured in an army household, frequent relocations taught him adaptability and seasoned in him the ability to build deeper and lasting connections with whoever he crossed paths with.

From his school days at Scindia school, where he developed the habit of introspection, to cultivating an innovative mindset at IIT Delhi, to honing a wide range of professional skills at L&T, DCM, and most importantly, HCL, and finally to founding NIIT, Pawar's journey has been nothing short of enlightening and inspiring.

And to honour his tireless pursuit of excellence, the nation decided to award him with the Padma Bhushan award in 2011, one of the most prestigious recognitions bestowed upon those who turn ideas into institutions, and institutions into legacies that only grow stronger with time.

He was the first one to address the increasing skill gap in the technology sector and laid the foundation of an institution that continues to empower countless young minds to build successful career paths in the world of technology.

Prajodh Rajan, Founder of Lighthouse Learning (Erstwhile 'Eurokids')

Preschool forms the foundation of a nation's growth, and Prajodh Rajan has played an invaluable role in transforming the way the parents and teachers perceive India's preschool landscape. What was merely seen as a preparatory stage for primary schooling has now become a fundamental pillar in an individual's growth, thanks to the revolution Rajan sparked through his vision with Eurokids.

Coming from a long lineage of educators, Rajan deeply admired the dedication and transformative role teachers play in nurturing young minds. Probably why the universe conspired to steer him away from the corporate world and towards his true calling—education. Through Eurokids, Euroschools and other preschool and K-12 initiatives, he ensured his work touched the lives of both—children and the change drivers who guide them.

What truly made his network of schools a trusted brand among parents are its unmatched pillars—child-first philosophy, thoughtfully designed and curiosity-driven curriculum, and exceptional safety protocols. Above all, its owner-operated franchise model has empowered countless women entrepreneurs, enabling them to redefine their career paths while shaping the lives of thousands of young minds.

Looking ahead, Rajan through his parent company, Lighthouse Learning, aims to expand beyond preschool and K-12 education landscape to transform higher education as well, paving the way for a brighter and more inclusive future for learners of all ages.

These visionaries have shaped children's minds, built lasting institutions, reshaped policies, enabled systemic shifts in the ecosystem, all the while, staying true to the purpose of Education.

Their lessons are never needed more than now, when AI is reshaping jobs and students, teachers and institution builders are worrying not just how to teach better, but what to teach and how learning can really make their students be ready for a dramatically shifting future.

SECTION 1

Changing Foundations

The early years of our education shape our future. Foundational skills—the ability to read and calculate—perhaps seemingly simple but if not addressed early, make learning an uphill journey for many students in later years.

Meanwhile, giving children an environment where they thrive and learn to build curiosity, resilience and cognitive skills, is the true gift of education.

In this section, read the stories of the visionaries who have been able to build the solid foundations of education's emerging blueprint in our nation.

CHAPTER 1

The 'I CAN' Revolution: Children as Changemakers

Kiranbir Sethi, Founder of Riverside School and Design For Change

'One child empowered, a generation transformed'

EARLY INFLUENCES PLANTED THE SEEDS OF CURIOSITY AND RAISED A DESIGN THINKER

In many Indian families, children are often silenced with phrases like 'You can't do this', 'This is not your age to question', 'Girls shouldn't do such things', or 'It is not safe for you.' But, in a liberal home in Bangalore, a different narrative was unfolding—one that was nurturing not just a design thinker but an original thinker—Kiranbir Sethi. In a world obsessed with restricting children with textbook rules and age-old beliefs, she chose an unconventional path. Not only did she become an educator, but a changemaker, empowering children in turn to break free from rigid norms and to embrace creative expression.

The youngest of the three children, Sethi's father was a trailblazer with numerous accolades to his name—India's first machine tool designer, a gold medallist, and a part of the first graduating batch of IIT Kharagpur. Beyond his professional brilliance, he was a curious soul—a painter at heart and a true lover of life. It was his zest that deeply influenced Sethi's life.

'I have some of the best memories growing up,' she recalls. 'We grew up without television and with just one phone in the house. It was that moment of just simplicity, school and play. We always used to tell stories at the dinner table. That was a very strong ritual at home. I had a maverick childhood.'

Much of what later shaped Sethi's core principles and values can be traced back to her early years. Raised in a closely-knit family, she never encountered gender-based biases at home. Though she went to Bishop Cotton Girls' High School, a traditional institute, most of her enlightening experiences were fuelled by the progressive mindset of her family.

For instance, at the age of twelve, during a school project on the study of life forms, Sethi's class was divided into groups, each asked to pick an organism to study. While others chose simpler organisms, Sethi very boldly proposed that her group study snakes. This wasn't a theoretical assignment; it involved purchasing a snake, bringing it home for observation, feeding it as required and monitoring it closely. In most households, such a suggestion would have been immediately dismissed. She got surprised when her family agreed to support her.

'I took Rs 2 from each group member, so I had a princely sum of Rs 20,' Sethi recalls emphasizing the naturally supportive environment she was brought up in. ***'Back then, there was a Yellow Pages book, and right at the end was this ad of a gentleman who used to be a wildlife preserver. So, I called him up and he said, "Yes, I have a snake." Then I called my papa and said, "Papa we have to buy a snake." My father and mother immediately said, "Okay we will go." I realized that that moment could have immediately ended with a "Are you mad? You want to get a snake?". But there they were. My mad father with an equally mad mother, ready to drive all the way to the other end of Bangalore to get it.'***

That particular moment became foundational in Sethi's belief that if you have an idea, you can pursue it. Her family's willingness to entertain her curiosity instilled in her a deep sense of agency, cementing her confidence in her own abilities. This supportive upbringing continued well beyond her childhood. Whether it was her decision to enrol in NID (National Institute of Design) right after clearing her 11th grade or getting married even before her elder sister, an unusual sight in many households, her family never questioned her choices. If she was ready, that was enough for them to lend their full support.

In essence, a series of such choices taught Sethi that purpose, confidence and competence were all she needed to chase any dream. It was the planting of this mindset that set the stage for a visionary leader—one that was destined to transform the landscape of K-12 education in India.

THE NID YEARS: WHEN DESIGN MET PURPOSE

After completing her schooling and spending one year at Mount Carmel College, Sethi finally stepped into the spectacular world of National Institute of Design, Ahmedabad.

'***I think it was possibly my tryst with NID that awakened everything that I had to know. NID was really a game changer for me; that first year was full of life and learning. Learning from your seniors, teachers, library, kaka at the chai galla ... there was a freedom and exploration of life into yourself. I think those years really put the blueprint of Riverside.***'

From the more traditional schooling that she had experienced till then, she was stunned by the 'alive and challenging' atmosphere of NID. It demanded participation and introduced her to the power of 'what if'. It was there that she understood that design is not just about aesthetics but rather addressing problems with creativity and empathy. This learning laid the bricks of her emerging belief system: design can transform lives if crafted keeping the end user in mind.

The way the institute operated, taught and carried out assessments initially baffled her. Having grown up with predetermined written tests based on textbooks, she was unprepared for NID's unique jury process, where students presented their work in front of jury and faculty members. Along with assessing the content presented by the students, these test procedures helped cultivate crucial skills, including negotiation and clear communication which were designed to boost confidence.

Though Sethi adapted to the jury process at the age of seventeen; today, children at her own school, Riverside, embrace it as early as age seven. This is one of the many powerful systems and ideologies that she brought with her NID education, a testament to how deeply those years influenced her.

Even during her semester breaks, when she thought she would finally get some rest, her father would encourage to visit his factory instead, urging her to consider it her playground, and so she did.

'Going to the shop floor, working with the workers, sandpapering, and going into the blue printing machine. It was that we all were working at the factory, there was no distinction between my work and play, we just worked. Work was a huge part of growing up, but having the joy in work came from seeing my family and later, my husband. It taught me that work could be a powerful way of engaging with life.'

It was also during these years that she grasped a core insight: design wasn't just a tool to execute ideas; it was the way of life.

While completing her graduation, Sethi faced a profound personal loss, the passing of her father. Her father's death left her with a lasting lesson: the importance of living in the present and not postponing what matters. It is a philosophy she continues to apply both in her professional and personal life, nurturing relations with intention. The final six months at NID were particularly challenging. Alongside grieving her father, she also got married, a period of emotional upheaval and transition. As a result, she found herself distracted and unable to give full focus to her academic work. When the time came to submit her final project, she admits that she didn't do justice to it, ***'I did a shoddy job,'*** she candidly reflects.

Considering the change of events, her mentor and jury member, Mukesh Patel, could have easily let her pass by allowing her to bluff her way through the project. But he didn't. Instead, he held his ground, ***'Kiran, it cannot work like this. You have to redo. Integrity to the idea and process is non-negotiable.'*** Had he let her off the hook, she believes she would have lost respect, not only for herself but for him as well. His harsh stance, though hard to hear at the time, left her feeling deeply grateful. It was this lesson in accountability, integrity and honest feedback that she treasures and remains guided by.

Post NID, Sethi set out on her path and opened her own firm, operating as an experience designer. Her first project was designing a restaurant called 'Mirch Masala' in Ahmedabad, owned by a friend. It was here that she first learned the power of storytelling through space—how every element could be used to curate an experience for the customers. Driven by passion, she used every opportunity to experiment and push her creative boundaries.

For instance, on Fridays that fell on the 13th, they would convert the restaurant into a 'Bhoot Bangla' playing into the horror theme, and during festivals, she would ask staff to become different avatars of Amitabh Bachchan and other celebrities to entertain the customers. These playful experiments allowed her to experience flexibility in her creative thinking, enabling her to generate solutions without the fear of failure.

EDUCATION REIMAGINED: THE RIVERSIDE SCHOOL BORN FROM EMPATHY AND BUILT WITH PURPOSE

Married to Geet Sethi, a nine-time World Billiard champion, she first-hand saw the power of deep dedication and commitment to unwavering excellence.

Sethi's perspective on education took a sharp turn just three months into her son, Raag's, first year of schooling. One day, he returned home with a punishment slip for the 'grave' mistake of writing one sentence before the other. He asked her to sign it, nervously, fearing that any sign of defiance might lead to further reprimands. Sethi could sense his anxiety, a feeling born not from learning but from the rigid system demanding obedience over understanding.

That moment stayed with her. In fact, it deepened during a parents-teacher meeting, where Raag's teacher couldn't even recall his name. For her, that was the point of saturation. She realized that the system was suppressing the growth of young minds, valuing 'compliance over conversation and passivity over curiosity.'

Her close involvement in her son's life made it clear: had she let him continue unquestionably in that environment, he would have grown into an obedient child—disciplined, yes, but disconnected from his own voice and joy. His 'I Can' mindset would have gradually transitioned to a hesitant 'Can I?'- a transformation that could have put not only his childhood, but entire existence at risk.

She had two options: change his school and hope for a better experience or accept the system as it was and eventually make peace with it. She chose neither. The designer in her couldn't settle for quick fixes and band-aid solutions. Hence, she carved out the third path: challenging the status quo and redesigning the system itself. Drawing on the design principles she had learned at NID, she set out on a journey to create an alternative learning environment where the students, actual 'users' could feel seen and heard. An environment where learning took precedence over marks and degrees. Her unshakable belief that education should empower students to become curious, capable, and humane citizens led to the birth of the 'Riverside School' in 2001.

Even the name 'Riverside' reflected the culture of creativity and inclusivity. Originally, Sethi had named the school 'Takshashila', inspired by the ancient Indian centre of learning, known for its holistic approach to education. But when she noticed young students struggling to pronounce it, she asked them to suggest an alternative. One child innocently pointed out, 'Ma'am, we are next to a river.' And just like that the name 'Riverside' was born—simple, relevant and chosen by the very students it was created for.

But was the journey easy? Absolutely not! As a designer with no formal background in education, Sethi had to start from scratch. She travelled across the world, visiting some of the top schools to observe, interview teachers, unabashedly ask questions and learn firsthand how learning environments could be transformed. Most importantly, she adopted reading as her mantra to drive change. She immersed herself into the educational theories of visionaries like J. Krishnamurti, Gijubhai Badheka, Reggio Emelia, and her personal favourite, Dr Howard Gardner. However, what truly led to the success of Riverside was the idea: *you never design for the user, you design with the user.*

On 26 January 2001, precisely at 8:40 a.m., the very first day of Riverside was set to launch, everything came crashing down, quite literally. A devastating 8.0 magnitude earthquake that had struck Gujarat, shook not just the ground beneath them but also the confidence of many parents who had expressed interest in the school's unconventional learning model. While the school building withstood tremors, it paused Sethi's journey even before she had started. But she didn't stop. Instead, the disaster gave her a new lens: she realized that to reimagine and rebuild education, she would require unmatched resilience and strength to survive several earthquakes—literal and metaphorical. That day she gave her own 'I Can' test and passed with flying colours.

Since then, she has never looked back. Her journey has only expanded, evolving from designer to educator, author, TED Talk expert and global social entrepreneur. Along the way, she has achieved several awards and recognition for her unwavering commitment to making education more student-centric and purpose-driven.

THE DESIGN PROCESS IN EDUCATION: BUILT FOR STUDENTS, CO-CREATED WITH THEM

Empathy as The Key Ingredient in the Recipe For Success

In her 2023 book *Every Child Can*, Sethi describes how Riverside School has harnessed the design process to reimagine every facet of school life—from pedagogy and teacher training to timetabling, parent-school relationships, and school and community engagements. At the heart of this transformative process, she emphasizes on a critical element: empathy. It is the driving force behind every design decision. In this empathy driven-model, children take the centre stage, not the curriculum.

Take, for instance, the Home Visit Process, where the Riverside team visits each student's home annually to avoid making assumptions about a child's learning. This idea stemmed from a moment that deeply moved Sethi. One day, a student casually mentioned that his mother didn't allow him to play outside much. Furious, Sethi decided to connect with the family to question them. What she discovered was revealing: the family's modest apartment was situated on a busy, traffic-filled street with no garden in the neighbourhood. Yet, the home was full of warmth, laughter and lots of indoor games.

This instilled a powerful lesson in Sethi and her team: the true power of the design process lies in keeping 'who and why' above 'what and how'. It is one of the many instances, where Sethi addressed her own elephants in the room to ensure Riverside never slipped into the framework of conventional Indian schools.

The FIDS Framework: Action Oriented, User-Centric Design Thinking Process

At NID, Sethi learned the five-step design process: empathize, define, ideate, prototype, and test. To her, this felt intuitive while creating various procedures and processes at Riverside. However, to her team, it seemed complex and intimidating. Recognizing the need to simplify and democratize the process, she with her team, turned the process into a simple four-step 'FIDS' framework: *Feel, Imagine, Do, and Share.* '***We use FIDS everywhere and everything, from designing spaces and curriculum to developing policies for recruitment and retention, from planning experiences and excursions to timetabling'*** she wrote in her book.

- **Feel: To create better solutions; it's important to empty your mind of all assumptions. One must carefully observe, engage and research.**
- **Imagine: To brainstorm and imagine the change you wish to see; but not alone, collaborate with others.**
- **Do: Create a prototype and develop a strategic plan, bridging together intention and action to successfully implement the act of change.**
- **Share: Harness the power of inspiration to create a greater impact. Share the story of change to inspire others into believing that 'they can' achieve their dreams.**

At Riverside, 'client projects' are an integral part of every student's curriculum—a dynamic bridge between classroom learning and real-world challenges. Unlike conventional education models where case studies are imaginative or extra coursework, Sethi has imbibed it within the academic framework. Rooted in FIDS, these projects shape children to be problem-solvers and change-makers from a young age.

Each project begins with a client from the Sethi's network giving students an opportunity to address their pain points and develop meaningful solutions by collaborating among each other. To keep a steady stream of clients always available, Sethi has collaborated with parents, city officials and leveraged her global network. On average, as stated in her book, a client project lasts for four to six weeks, requiring a minimum of five hours of work every week.

A standout example of the school's client projects was a collaboration between the school's tenth grade students and Havmor, Gujarat's leading ice cream brand. The company approached them with a brief: develop a special ice-cream flavour for the Christmas season. Applying the FIDS framework, students began with analyzing customer preferences, pricing strategy of company's best-selling products and gaining insights around marketing strategies.

Next, they envisioned what they wanted to achieve: the product becoming a permanent part of Havmor's menu. Keeping that in mind, they rolled up their sleeves, working at the ice cream factory, developing prototypes through multiple iterations and developing a full-fledged financial model including marketing plans and budgets. When they presented it to the company's owner, Pradeep Chona, he was astounded. Having seen countless presentations from MBA students, he expressed that what these schoolchildren had achieved was far more impressive not just generating a concept but delivering an actual, market-ready product.

Out of the many versions presented, the winning design was a festive delight—an inverted chocolate-covered cone with vanilla and raspberry swirls, topped with sprinkles to replicate Christmas decorations. They named it Razzmatazz. Just as they had envisioned, it became a part of Havmor's permanent menu. Today, FIDS has become a tool of empowerment for the students, giving them the liberty, voice and the right set of opportunities and agency to take charge of their own growth.

Developing Curriculum With Conscience: Aligning Rigor, Relevance, and Experiential Learning

Based on her own schooling experience and that of her children, Sethi was clear on one thing: She didn't want Riverside to follow a conventional curriculum as it prioritized grades above learning and growth. She believed that when a student's potential is reduced to the numbers on his report card, they start equating their self-worth with their marks. The message 'If I don't get good marks, I'm not good enough' becomes internalized, risking their mental well-being. Sethi was determined to break this vicious cycle.

Taking every aspect into consideration, she developed a curriculum that is a perfect balance of rigorous academic preparation and student-centric learning approaches. While the school affiliates with ICSE and IGCSE board requirements, she made sure not to compromise her core belief: children learn best when they are engaged and deeply connected with what they study. The curriculum is not considered as a rigid syllabus to be completed but rather a flexible framework, one that allows room for creativity, critical thinking, compassion and collaboration. Academic concepts are woven into real-world projects and experiential learning, allowing them to understand not just what they are learning but also why it matters and how to apply it in meaningful ways.

This approach ensures that students perform exceptionally well academically and shape up to becoming curious and compassionate human beings. However, convincing the parents and the community for the school's non-conformity to age-old norms wasn't easy for Sethi. Especially when in 2012, a batch of students received the result for their AS-levels (11th grade) which left the teachers stunned and parents angry as the grades were quite low. What followed was the criticism from parents towards the curriculum and push for the school to adopt the 'teach for the test' model.

However, Sethi didn't succumb to the pressure but instead reimagined the timetable to give equal importance to academic mastery and character development. Since Cambridge Board allows students to re-test, teachers followed the newer model and as expected, students exceeded the expectations. Each year, Riverside students continue to outperform their peers from ten other schools in the ASSET exam, proving that the school's empowering curriculum not only nurtures a student's personal growth but also ensures strong academic performance.

But what happens to the curriculum and processes when teachers leave, new ones get hired, and different batches of students and parents join Riverside? How does Sethi stick to her core beliefs and intent without imposing her narrative on the new joinees? The answer is documentation and codification. Since the very first year, she learned the importance of documentation and codification of processes to help each teacher, or a parent, understand why the process was started and the intent behind it. Most importantly, documentation saved time, simplified the adaptation and made it easier to share and iterate as required.

MOVING THE 'I CAN' MINDSET BEYOND THE CLASSROOM

The aProCh Initiative: Bringing Together Students and Adults to Create Children-Friendly Cities

After returning from her study tour of Reggio Emilia approach in Italy, Sethi shared her notice of how the Italian city prioritized its children—offering them safe spaces. This conversation between her and her students, sparked the idea for the aProCh—acronym for 'A Protagonist in every Child'-initiative, a city-based movement to design Indian cities to be friendlier for children, in 2007.

However, introducing the initiative first required navigating a maze of permissions from the government officials. For the inaugural program, 'Street Smart', the team had to persuade and negotiate with the city commissioner to close the 'Law Garden' street for one single day. Initially skeptical, the commissioner agreed, viewing it as a one-off event. Led by a dynamic team of students, business minds, designers and professors, the event turned out to be a success. It featured tri-colour ice creams, spontaneous dance classes, skater and balloon artists, magic shows, cricket matches, flag hoisting and most importantly, the first-ever child-friendly zebra crossing.

Besides this, Sethi also launched Movie-ing Experience, an initiative that encourages multiplexes and cinema halls to open their doors to most vulnerable children each month, offering them the opportunity to enjoy the full theatre experience (including popcorn!). This was followed by various others: 'Parents of the Park' and 'City as My Landscape', each designed to empower and engage the community in meaningful ways.

Though it wasn't easy, Sethi believes every ounce of effort was it. Along with convincing several key police officials, they often faced unfulfilled promises from volunteers, anger from residents, and low morale whenever they encountered insults. Despite all of it, they remain undeterred, showing up time and again to carry out their initiatives and give back to the community, continuing to show up and carry out the initiatives. Their years of perseverance paid off as in 2023, they celebrated their fifteenth anniversary.

Design for Change (DFC): From FIDS Framework at School to a Revolutionary Global Movement

In 2009, a friend approached Sethi to launch an ambitious idea he had brewed with his friends—celebrating a week of giving around Gandhi Jayanti. She loved the concept but proposed 'What if children were to understand the importance of sharing and giving through this initiative?' That's how 'Design for Change' was born. Drawing insights and learnings from aProCh initiative, Sethi was excited to see her students turning into role models and inspiring hundreds of others. However, she knew that to invite participation from schools across the nation, the name 'Riverside' wouldn't suffice. So, she partnered with her friends from IDEO and Stanford's Design School, and enlisted her sister, Poonam, who was also an NID graduate, to design self-explanatory toolkits for students.

Initially, Sethi thought that even if 500 schools participated, she would be more than happy. But after leveraging her network, she ended up printing around 30,000 toolkits in eleven Indian languages. Slowly, after a few weeks, stories of change started knocking their doors, each a testament that transformation was happening in diverse and meaningful ways. '***From Jhunjhunu in the north-west to Hyderabad in the south; from Sikkim in the north-east and Nashik in the south-west—from stopping child marriages to caring for the elderly, from tackling bullying to reducing the weight of school bags—the solutions from elegant and impactful. In all, we got over 900 stories of change,' Sethi wrote in her book.***

That same year, Sethi was invited at the TED India conference in Mysore to share the inspiring story of Riverside. Once her TED talk went live on the company's official website, her narrative went viral. It became a turning point that metamorphosed the Design for Change initiative into a global movement. Her first international invitation came from a teacher in Taiwan who, moved by her story, requested her to come to Taiwan and introduce the initiative to her students.

A major leap in scaling the initiative came from the Vatican's desire to adopt the 'I Can' philosophy, leading to embedment of DFC in all the catholic schools across the globe. This particular strategy became one of the largest education movements in the world.

Today, DFC is in over sixty-five countries and is continuously growing by bringing together leaders, social entrepreneurs, designers and educators, who are strictly committed to the 'I Can' mindset. At heart, DFC is not about solving problems on a global level, it's about turning students into enablers with agency, voice, and purpose.

THE WAY AHEAD: EMPOWERMENT IS AN ONGOING JOURNEY

In 2001, when Sethi pulled her son Raag out of his school, she only had two things in mind: voice and choice. She made her choice and launched Riverside School with the purpose of giving children a voice. Everything was going well until 2008, when a student, Kartikeya, shared a deeply unsettling observation, that students were tying their self-worth to academic performance to the point where failure in exams was leading some to take their own lives. That moment pushed Sethi to expand her mission and design an identity curriculum, a framework that would help students view their identities beyond grades, and nurture a more holistic sense of self.

Her Design for Change and aProCH initiatives have amplified her vision on global platforms, urging the educators worldwide harness the power of education for instilling the 'I Can' mindset in every child and empowering them. Additionally, the launch of Riverside Learning Center has been pivotal in offering guidance to every other school to adopt the design thinking model and other processes that assisted Riverside nurture confident and compassionate students.

Looking forward, Sethi continues to see herself not just as an educator but a designer of change. Someone who continuously questions the status quo, evolves with purpose, and learns from the actual changemakers—children. As Riverside and its offshoots continue to explore new domains in need of improvement, Sethi's North Star remains consistent—to nurture a generation of problem-solvers who can steer the world forward with clarity and conviction.

CHAPTER 2

Lessons Rooted in Faith, Guided by Values

Grace Pinto and Family, Founder of Ryan International Schools

'Education nurtures believers, before achievers'

FOUNDATION OF A PASSIONATE EDUCATOR—EARLY LIFE INFLUENCES AND CHALLENGES

Across Indian households, the name Ryan International has garnered immense trust, standing tall not just as any educational institution but one where children are nurtured and offered a value-based education. Behind Ryan's grandeur, is the unwavering dedication and unmatched vision of its founder, Grace Pinto—a woman who set out on a journey to transform the K-12 education landscape of India along with her husband Dr Augustine F. Pinto.

Grace was raised in Mangalore from a humble background, with her father working as a driver in Dubai and her mother taking care of the family as a homemaker. Her education in a convent school planted the seeds of inspiration as she observed the nuns' dedication, devotion and determination to provide premium quality education wrapped in moral values and religious discipline.

After her marriage to Dr Pinto, whom she credits as the true visionary behind Ryan, Grace got deeply inspired to become a teacher.

'Dr Pinto is the real visionary. I assisted him. The journey was very tough. There is no godfather, only Lord Jesus Christ is our mentor and guide, and Mother Terresa is my role model. She is the reflection of Jesus Christ. She had come all the way to India and worked for the underprivileged. So, I said, "Why can't I also do something?"'

When Grace moved to Bombay, she began to see the potential in herself and gained the confidence to start her journey. Together, they crystalized the idea of starting their own school—an institution where they could bring their vision to life by nurturing young talent.

In the 1970s, when they were just beginning their journey as educators, education was nowhere near to what it is today. There were no schools in suburbs of Mumbai, which sparked the idea in the Pintos to take matters into their own hands and start a school that could instil in young minds the finest of educational, intellectual, and behavioural values.

Grace was a little sceptical initially as they neither had the money nor a piece of land to lay the foundation for a school. 'To start the school, we required a building and comprehensive support. Every type of facility and resource was essential', She recalls. Dr Pinto's dedication led him to an ideal place, luckily available for rent, but money was still a concern.

This is where Grace stepped in, giving away every piece of gold she had received from her parents as a wedding gift. At the same time, banks and fund lending institutions played a crucial role in bringing their vision to life. The couple approached these institutions not as profit-driven entrepreneurs, but as visionaries committed to public good. While financing educational institutions was far from easy during those years, their conviction earned trust. Their own beliefs, combined with the trust of the lenders, allowed them to plant the seeds of what would eventually grow into India's largest school network.

In 1976, the couple rented the land for the seeding phase, a period focused on laying the operational framework and engaging in the experimentation. However, the real breakthrough happened in 1983 when Dr Pinto and Grace launched their first school, St. Xavier's High School, in Borivali, Mumbai. This marked the true beginning of a prosperous journey. Not only did the parents place their trust in the couple's abilities, but the banks were also quick to expedite the approval process and extend the necessary loans. During these intervening years, Grace also embraced motherhood, giving birth to three children, two daughters and a son.

Even as early as the 1970s, a time when getting education was considered a luxury, Grace was striving for something different. Dr Pinto and she felt the need to introduce children to the idea of learning while paying equal emphasis on holistic development of children. Their focus was on ensuring that their school didn't join the monotonous path of rote subject teaching. Not long after launching their first school, St. Xavier's, they began opening more than four schools each year, creating a chain of premium-quality institutions in Mumbai and its suburbs.

Despite her unshakable dedication and hard work, Grace gives complete credit to God for being her mentor and guide through many challenges she faced. From financial struggles to envy from competitors, her journey has been far from seamless. Yet, she never lost faith and trust in God, and till today, credits Him for helping her navigate the unforeseen.

EXPANSION TO NEW CITY—THE OFFICIAL BIRTH OF RYAN INTERNATIONAL

After firmly establishing themselves in Mumbai and by 1991, they began receiving invitations from Delhi. However, this shift from Mumbai to Delhi, was more than just a geographical transition, it represented embracing a new identity, something modern and global.

At that time, the national capital was evolving into a melting pot of cultures. This called for Pintos to rebrand their institutions under a new banner, a name that echoed Indian values but aligned with global standards. This marked the birth of Ryan Group of Institutions.

'In Delhi, an officer remarked that 'Saint' would not be acceptable and suggested choosing another appealing name. That's when I thought "Why not use my son's name'?"

Named after their son, Ryan Pinto, this brand carried a broader appeal, helping the institution build an inclusive reputation—their vision had always been to expand across the globe, starting with their country. This strategic move made it much easier for the brand to build forward in different states of India, avoiding the limitations that a religiously overt and conventional name might have posed. What started as a family-run mission, eventually grew into a nationwide movement, with Ryan becoming synonymous with a school known for offering modern, value-based education.

While they had already established a reputation as a CBSE-affiliated school in Delhi, Grace made sure to adapt to the international teaching standards. As a result, she introduced ICSE, ICS, SSC and IB curricula by obtaining all the required permissions from the state. Doing so helped meet the changing demands of education by offering children more choice. But behind this strategic growth was not just a sound educational philosophy but also a powerful partnership. While Dr Pinto scheduled expansions and laid the early bricks, Grace brought the structure and strategy to sustain momentum.

'Dr Pinto was very highly enterprising and driven, always envisioning the expansion of more schools. You can say, I was responsible for translating those ideas into practice.'

Dr Pinto focused on logistical areas such as identifying regions for expansion, engaging with builders, seeking approvals from banks, and navigating legal battles—ultimately creating a solid framework for each school. Whereas Grace Pinto became the face as well as force behind the uninterrupted success of the institution.

As a managing director, she took over the administrative control in a way that ensured standardizing quality across all the schools under the brand, blending curriculum with spiritual and moral belief system, promoting co-curricular activities, and most importantly, building an uninterrupted teacher training procedure.

Grace's deep involvement in school functions, interaction with parents, value-led mindset, and public representation, made her a respected leader in the space of education. Together, the Pintos ensured that Ryan didn't just grow in numbers but expanded in depth and distinctiveness, upholding its promise to nation-building. Though their partnership grew as a force driving a massive change in the education landscape of India, Grace admits that her deepest sacrifice was with precious time she could have spent with her children during their childhood days.

'My children made significant sacrifices because I was unable to give them the time they deserved. The journey was challenging but I remained committed and dedicated everything to Jesus. I devoted more time to schools, often at the cost of personal occasions. There were times when I

couldn't take part in celebrations. Dr Pinto advised me "Set aside anniversaries and celebrations for now—focus on your work." I followed that guidance, and it is through that dedication that we have reached where we are today.'

With each expansion of Ryan International Group, Grace found herself immersed in a pile of responsibilities. From overseeing school operations, to training staff, attending public events, and building a great network.

She nurtured thousands of children who grew under her guidance, in her schools, making sure to instil the right values in them. Her children saw her as more than just their mother, but also as a leader with a purpose, and this sense of commitment-driven legacy continues to motivate the next generation.

A Glimpse of a Typical Day in Grace's Everyday Life as The Managing Director

A typical day in Grace Pinto's life started with visiting schools, where she made it a point to meet and connect with children, staff, and principals. She believed that while leaders may carry a strong vision, it is the people around them who put things into practice. Her routine was not about oversight but about building deep connections; listening to concerns, offering words of encouragement, and ensuring that everyone felt heard and supported. Grace understood that leadership wasn't about directing people to move in a particular direction, but about instilling faith in them so that they could confidently discover their own directions.

FINDING THE RIGHT TEACHERS AND CURATING THE RIGHT TEACHING PHILOSOPHY

From the very beginning of their journey, Pintos knew that the success of a school heavily relied on the teachers it recruited. No matter how strong the vision, how immaculate the infrastructure, or how engaging the curriculum may be, they were aware that it was the teachers who truly guided the children. They believed that teachers were not just the conveyors, but the true custodians of the founding values and mission of the founders. Hence, recruiting teachers was a process they approached with deep personal involvement, a practice that could change the professional landscape of India if cultivated.

While they considered the applicants educational background important, they valued how the teachers understood and aligned with the vision of the school more. To serve their purpose, they hand-picked each teacher. Around ninety of their principals started as kindergarten teachers in Ryan but eventually rose to esteemed designations under the tutelage of Grace Pinto.

Like her students, Grace ensured that teachers continued to grow through ongoing training and support from the department.

'We encouraged teachers to pursue further studies even after joining. We supported them in completing their training and provided assistance through our department. We also implemented an undertaking requiring teachers

to continue their professional development after being employed at Ryan Schools. As a result, teachers were able to complete their education, and we built a strong, well-qualified team.'

Ryan Pinto, the current CEO, recalls his initial days when he would carefully observe how his mother approached the hiring process, often jotting down notes on a piece of paper. He believes that his mother's talent of identifying the right people for the job is purely God's gift.

She would spend time with teachers, train them, and take them for visits to other schools to gain broader perspectives.

Along with meticulously identifying the best possible teachers for her schools, Grace gave equal amount of attention to curating a well-rounded and effective curriculum. Along with drawing inspiration from her own time at a convent school, she visited a lot of schools to be able to get the needed clarity about what was being offered and what the students needed.

Besides, her networking had led to a lot of friends in the education sector who also lent a hand. From her own experience, she knew that schools only focused on books and exams. Not much attention was given to other areas of excellence such as sports, drama, interactions, thoughts and innovation, which often deprived young minds from developing the right set of life skills.

Her aim was to offer a holistic learning experience to every child who stepped into Ryan. As a result, they included a wide range of extra-curricular activities and life skills programs to ensure that each child became an all-rounder, equipped to excel in multiple areas, something the parents were appreciative of. For instance, the school-organized International Theatre Festival allowed children to learn in-depth about different countries, their problems, day-to-day work, and their economic as well as social stance.

This further helped the institution to draw parents' attention and set benchmarks for other institutions. In other words, what they started almost twenty years back after thorough experimentation and research, has now become a standard practice. But what's even more staggering to know is that while other institutions were beginning to follow in their footsteps, Ryan decided to go ten notches higher by increasing the visibility of their festivals. Now, this annual festival takes place as a week-long program in two metropolitan cities, Mumbai and Delhi, where 20,000-25,000 students participate from fifteen to twenty countries.

Additionally, their emphasis on sports is not to be looked over. Each year, numerous sporting events are conducted across all the Ryan schools in India, helping children to interact and explore with like-minded peers and seniors. Today, Ryan students represent India in multiple sports, including cricket, football, and badminton. Notably, three 'Ryanites' who won medals in the last Asian Games held in China (2023) are a testament to the impact these programs have created and how they have facilitated children in discovering their own talents.

Grace has always been very encouraging of technology adoption and innovation. So, when computers arrived in the 1990s with Google, St Xavier's, the first official school started by Pintos, was the first in Mumbai to establish a computer lab. Though initially, concern was raised as parents thought that the school would convert their children into typists, Grace held on to her stance and pushed parents to trust them and their methodologies. As she used to continuously travel abroad, she was always eager to bring the best practices and technologies to her own institutions. But they didn't stop there!

Pintos developed an unprecedented idea—to set a faculty-chosen full-fledged school parliament, where students would be the cabinet members and take on positions like vice president, president, and prime minister. So, from education, to transport, health, and finance, all these ministers are represented in the school parliament. They are taught in terms of diplomacy and responsibility.

For example, Ryan Pinto highlights how during the monsoon season, the environment ministers of the school become very busy to tackle the challenges that come with heavy rainfall. Similarly, transport ministers in the school can be seen continuously writing to local civic bodies.

Moreover, they continuously carry various student-led programs, including plantation drives, environmental drives, and health initiatives to promote community building.

Every year, each Ryan school is mandated to work with five NGOs in their local community. The student council chooses the NGOs, but most of them cater to the children of the underserved community, orphanages, and old age homes as these are long-term, purpose-driven engagements and not a mere tick in the box. Moreover, the institution deliberately avoids publicizing such initiatives as their purpose is not popularity, they already have plenty of it. Their true purpose is impact.

'While we teach our children academics, our greatest joy comes from seeing them grow into good, responsible human beings who contribute positively to society in their own ways. Not everyone will become the CEO of a unicorn, and that's perfectly fine. Whatever career path one chooses, true success is impossible without being a good human first. This belief is deeply woven into our teaching and learning process.'

Alongside offering the opportunities to grow through various programs and initiatives across a spectrum of areas, Ryan Institution strictly emphasizes on the elements of self-discovery by introducing children to numerous values and beliefs—spiritual, ethical, and religious—which the Pinto family has always strongly upheld.

Also, the unmatched dedication of the Pinto family is still intact. Each year, they meet every final year student, around 25,000 students at their farewell. But before that, they engage in another event, Team Camp, where final year students are invited to stay at campsites to help them relax and unwind.

As this is mostly their first trip away from family, it is a very special occasion for each student. Presence of Grace at the Camp is precisely to meet and spend meaningful time with the children who had spent sixteen years at Ryan, now ready to embark on their future educational and career journeys.

THE PROOF OF PURPOSE: SUCCESS STORIES THAT MADE OUT OF THE CLASSROOM

'We did a recent study from our alumni base. Out of eighteen IITs, we had at least one or two Ryan students enrolled in sixteen of them. Similarly, we looked at the top fifty colleges of India, and in all fifty, we found there were nearly five Ryan students enrolled there. Around 20,000 to 25,000 students graduate from Ryan each year and we have around a quarter million students studying with us today.'

The true success of Ryan reflects not in terms of the number of campuses built and technologies adopted but lives impacted. The success of its students long after they graduated shows how the values, beliefs, and teachings instilled helped them to carve out rewarding career paths. Ryan Pinto recalls many such faces who once thrived in the corridors of their schools and now are leading the world forward.

He remembers meeting one such young boy recently, who was one of the students from their Malad, Mumbai, branch. ***'He comes, and says "Sir, I'm already working" and towards the end of the conversation, he gives me his visiting card.' You know what the card said? Ministry of Finance.'*** In that very moment, Ryan felt an immense sense of pride looking at how far the boy had come in his professional journey.

One fine day, Ryan was coming back from one of his trips, and he sat next to a boy and got talking to him. Together they landed in Mumbai, and Ryan's uncle came to pick him up. When his uncle waved to Ryan, the boy he had sat next to on the plane said, 'Do you know that man?' To which Ryan responded with a casual 'Yeah!' The boy in absolute surprise said, 'How do you know Vinci Sir?'

Looking at that man, the boy's eyes immediately welled up. Ryan's uncle and that boy hugged and talked to each other for almost forty-five minutes. After they had bid goodbyes, his uncle informed Ryan that the boy was an ex-Ryanite, who's education had been sponsored by Grace and Dr Pinto since the boy was from a low-income background.

'Look at him today. From his father selling vegetables on the road to him living in Dubai, having his own business and travelling with you in business class. Look at the transformation.' These words of his uncle made Ryan realize how his parents had impacted thousands of lives.

Back in the 90s, many people started recognizing the increasing value of television and media. Normally, individuals were exposed to mass media and communication in college, however, Pintos wanted to bring the studio setup to their schools. Hence, a program called '*Ryan TV*' came into existence. This in-house studio allowed students, from grade six, to take up roles ranging from scripting, shooting, to editing and post-production. Every Sunday, the school had a thirty-minute program, managed completely by students, which was also televised on Zee channels. The same children are now working in so many renowned media houses, earning well-deserved respect and recognition.

Over the years, business leaders and corporate houses would often reach out to Grace and share that as soon as their HR teams saw candidates were Ryan alumni, they were immediately given preference. Why? Because the hiring teams understood how dedicated, diligent, and honest these individuals were. In essence, their strong core set them apart from the crowd.

While Ryan International has received several accolades and recognitions over the years, it is the stories of its alumni that stand as the truest testament of the impact created by Pintos. The journey of each Ryan student is a living proof that when the seed of purpose is planted and nurtured with care, it bears fruit for generations, further strengthening the roots and legacy of the tree from which it grew.

THE NEXT CHAPTER, CERTAINLY NOT THE LAST IN THE HISTORY OF RYAN—THE VISION FOR FUTURE

Nearly five decades after Grace and Dr Pinto laid the foundation for their dream, cemented with values and beliefs they upheld, Ryan International stands poised to carry its legacy into a new era, with a strong focus on technology and innovation. The next chapter combines traditional values with transformation, though the goal remains the same: to transform millions of lives by giving them access to value-led, premium-quality education.

'It took us fifty years to reach 150 campuses; my ambition is to establish the next hundred within the coming decade. To achieve this accelerated growth, we must deepen our presence in key regions across the country. We plan to

expand further into major metros, having recently ventured into Hyderabad, we see significant potential there. We also aim to strengthen our footprint in Bengaluru, Chennai and NCR markets. In addition, we are actively pursuing opportunities for further international expansion.'

Along with expanding its footprint in Indian and global markets, particularly UAE, Ryan Pinto is focused on using technology, both in terms of increasing efficiency of existing systems and leveraging it, to impact many more lives. Hence, he envisions moving education beyond just a brick-and-mortar setup. Moreover, he is clear that his primary role is to make sure that there is strengthening and continuity of the organization. So, in the future, when somebody asks the fourth generation of the Pinto Family, they should have it all planned.

On the other hand, Grace Pinto, the pillar holding the Ryan Institute together, intends to encourage and assist her son, Ryan in starting more schools under the banner to expand their vision. At the same time, she firmly believes that the future demands a stronger emphasis on technology, as times are changing rapidly, and education must keep pace with emerging trends, while keeping the mission of their institution intact.

CHAPTER 3

Weaving Wonder, Igniting Curiosity

Prajodh Rajan, Founder of Lighthouse Learning (Erstwhile 'Eurokids')

'Curiosity became curriculum, play became purpose.'

DEFINING TOMORROW—PRESCHOOL EDUCATION AS THE BEDROCK OF A NATION'S SUCCESS

'I have always believed that the future of a nation is decided long before its children enter formal schooling.'

For decades, education conversations in India focused on classrooms, curricula, and credentials that came much later in a child's life. Yet the most formative years—when curiosity is natural, imagination is boundless, and values quietly take root—remained underappreciated.

Studies in early childhood developed have conclusively established that nearly 85 percent of a child's brain development occurs before the age of six. But more than a statistic, early childhood education is about trust, emotional security, and joy. It is about how a child learns to wonder, to ask questions, to relate to the world, and to believe in themselves.

Preschool education in India was often viewed as optional, a place to keep children occupied rather than a space to nurture their potential. Parents hoped for care and safety, not as a foundation for learning and development. Teachers worked with passion but without structured support. And systems were fragmented, unorganised, and largely invisible in mainstream education policy.

However, India's preschool landscape has undergone a massive change over the last few years. Parents are now more aware that early education is a critical pillar for a child's cognitive, physical, social, emotional, and mental growth. This transformative shift in perception can be attributed to several factors, namely rapid urbanization, higher disposable incomes, rising nuclear families, and an increasing number of working parents.

What has further cemented parents' trust in early education is the method by which it is being imparted today. Gone are the days when preschools functioned like formal creches, offering a few hours of unstructured activities with minimal focus on learning. Modern preschools have interactive teaching methods, parent-teacher interactions, and progress updates—key components that contribute to a more structured, engaging, and holistic approach to early childhood education.

The NEP (National Education Policy) too has played a pivotal role in integrating early childhood education into the mainstream education system. The curricular structure 5+3+3+4 lays a strong emphasis on the foundational stage of learning, and activity-based learning in nurturing a child's potential and shaping their future.

Considering how this stage of education creates the groundwork for a child's academic and personal success, the demand for high-quality preschools is increasing exponentially. The numbers speak volumes; the Indian preschool market valued at $4.2 billion in 2023, is projected to skyrocket to $10.2 billion by 2032 exhibiting a growth rate (CAGR) of 10 per cent during 2024-2032. Clearly, India is on its way to becoming one of the world's largest markets for education, with the K-12 segment presenting an even bigger opportunity.

Prajodh Rajan's name defines the growth of this sector in the early 2000's. Since then, the market has witnessed stark growth, with many players following the same path to establish themselves in this evolving space.

PRAJODH RAJAN—FROM SCHOOL TO COLLEGE TO PROFESSIONAL WORLD: EACH PHASE SHAPING A VISIONARY LEADER

'Mom would say that this was always meant to be.'

What may seem like coincidence is often destiny's design and we are just players in its grand plan. Prajodh's journey into education wasn't entirely accidental. In fact, he wasn't the first one from his family to enter this space. His great grandfather served as the principal of an English-medium school, one of the first schools in Kerala, laying a legacy of learning and inspiration.

On the other hand, his maternal grandfather—a deeply spiritual man with a service-above-self mindset founded an ashram that included a school where Prajodh would often spend his summer breaks. Perhaps that's why, a lot of conversations in his home revolved around purpose, education, and the idea of giving back to the society, themes that quietly helped craft his path.

Growing up in such an environment, Prajodh often heard stories that deepened his belief in how teachers contributed to make the world a better place.

For his school education, Prajodh attended the same school where his mother taught. He went on to become the Vice-Captain and later the Captain of the school, focusing on enhancing his communication skills while continuing to excel in academics. His school also offered him the opportunities to explore plenty of other interests including science exhibitions, sports, drama, etc. These were not only opportunities; they were early lessons in empathy, leadership, and choice.

Beyond his own student leadership, it was the quiet observation of his mother's life as a teacher that left the deepest imprint on his journey. Watching her transition from a corporate career to a teaching profession and her tireless commitment to children Prajodh saw first-hand that teaching was far more than a profession; it was a profound calling. He witnessed the dedication required to shape young minds and realized that good quality education was the bedrock upon which all future success was built. He admits that much of his work and vision have been shaped by his early life experiences.

After acing his school years, Prajodh went on to pursue Aeronautical Engineering but dropped out after six months as his heart longed for work that felt more meaningful than physically strenuous. He went on to earn a BBA from Madras University inspired by his interest in management. He intended to pursue an MBA after three years of working; however his growing professional commitments kept him from doing so.

Prajodh began his career with a mobile telephony company, at a time when not many people in India had access to mobile phones, making his job the envy of many. Later, he joined a Japanese automobile company as part of the corporate sales team. During these initial years, he had two sales jobs and one marketing job, which taught him a great deal about start-ups and surviving through chaotic corporate environments.

It was during his stint at the automobile company that Prajodh met Vikas Phadnis, and they discovered a shared curiosity for business, innovation, and a sense of discipline. However, after a few years, Vikas moved to join a joint venture between Egmont, a Scandinavian publishing house, and an Indian newspaper publisher in the children's book publishing industry.

Recognizing the opportunity in this space, Vikas reached out to Prajodh inviting him to witness the incredible growth potential in the publishing business first-hand. However, at that time, Prajodh was content with his career trajectory and declined the offer.

That wasn't the end of their story, but rather a glimpse of what lay ahead.

A year later in 1999, Vikas made a renewed outreach to Prajodh to join Egmont, and he accepted the offer with the belief that Vikas had his best interest and saw an opportunity that he did not recognize initially.

While at Egmont, the primary focus was on children's book publishing and as part of a new distribution idea they wanted to provide content to pre-schools. However, they soon realized that the challenges facing early childhood education went far deeper than just lack of content. They observed that existing pre-schools were in dire need of a complete structural overhaul—from specialized teaching aids and resources to safe, child-friendly infrastructure. Recognizing that a curriculum could only be as effective as the environment in which it was taught, they pivoted from simply providing books to building a comprehensive nurturing ecosystem, which led to the birth of EuroKids.

In 2004, Egmont decided to focus on its core markets of Scandanavia and other European countries and decided to exit India along with other Asian markets. With their deep belief in the transformative power of early childhood education in shaping young minds, Prajodh along with his partners seized this opportunity and bought out Egmont's stake. That was when the company rebranded itself as EuroKids International Private Ltd, with a singular focus on revolutionizing preschool education in India.

EUROKIDS—A PLACE WHERE EARLY LEARNING FOUND ITS AUTHENTIC VOICE

'Our decision to enter the preschool space was driven by a clear need gap we identified back in 2001, when we were still publishing children's books. We saw that early education in India lacked an effective curriculum, age-appropriate learning requirements, and a strong value framework. This pushed us to move beyond content alone and commit to creating a robust, high-quality early childhood education ecosystem.'

In the early 2000s, preschool was largely viewed as a preparatory stage for formal schooling. Teachers and parents, focused on education only from grade 1, while pre-school became synonymous with playschool, leaving little attention to early developmental growth.

Enrolments were limited, and the primary focus remained on teaching basic alphabets and numbers, helping them adjust to school-like environments to ease their transition into the K-12 system.

The entire sector was highly unstructured and demanded immediate attention. Prajodh recognized the prevalent gap between the education sector and changing demands of the market. His mission was clear: to provide a nurturing and safe learning environment to kids. He gave his vision a brick-and mortar form in 2001 by opening two preschools in Mumbai, under the label 'EuroKids'. Prajodh also highlighted that the reason why the institution was called that was because the company at the time had a European connection and it was about kids, leading to its birth in India.

These exceptionally designed schools strictly followed a child-centric model to ensure a holistic development, gaining widespread recognition among parents. Back in 2002-2003, Prajodh built out a central education team, which included curriculum researchers, writers, and planners—an effort that continues to exist and drives the core principles of offering high quality education to young minds until today.

As the preschool landscape expanded and the competition intensified, Prajodh invested heavily behind enabling resources to upgrade the curriculum periodically. EuroKids maintained its market lead by successfully launching their eighth curriculum version named as "HEUREKA" in 2024. Deeply rooted in the child-first philosophy and built upon three foundational pillars of mindful learning, spaced learning, and blended learning, HEUREKA focuses on encouraging children to become aware of emotional regulation, ensuring spaced learning through frequent intervals for better retention, and combining traditional techniques with modern learning methods to create an enriching learning experience.

For Prajodh, curriculum was an act of respect—for childhood, curiosity, and the pace at which young minds naturally unfold.

Recognising the growing influence of technology in education, EuroKids has also incorporated digital tools such as the HomeBuddy app. The platform enables learning to continue beyond school hours through recorded lessons, interactive modules, and activities that deepen classroom understanding. With this approach, Prajodh and team have shaped HEUREKA into a curriculum that is not only nurturing but also progressive and deeply inclusive.

While curating a high-quality curriculum, Prajodh has remained steadfast in his 'Child First' philosophy, ensuring that every strategic decision prioritizes the well-being and safety of the learner. This commitment led him to pioneer the Safe School Protocol, where he partnered with one of the world's foremost assessment firms to audit and certify the network's safety standards. By placing the child's safety at the heart of the institutional design, he established EuroKids as India's first certified Safe School network, setting a new benchmark for health and safety standards in the country.

Each school adheres to stringent sixty-four points safety guidelines, including comprehensive staff background verification, CCTV monitoring, child-friendly infrastructure, and robust hygiene practices. This proactive approach has played a crucial role in earning the trust of the parents who were earlier hesitant to enrol their little ones in preschools due to safety concerns.

BUILDING A SUSTAINABLE AND SCALABLE BUSINESS MODEL—THE FRANCHISE STROKE OF GENIUS

'Back then 'franchising' was not a favourable word in India. I was truly inspired by McDonald's franchise system. I was amazed by how one could make and sell consistent products and processes across not just a nation but continents as well'

Many people insisted it wouldn't work in India and that quality would suffer. Prajodh listened, but trusted franchising as the model of growth for EuroKids, and this become the biggest reason why he has been able to build what he has built today.

After the success of EuroKids preschools in Mumbai, the need to expand and reach students across India led to the development of their iconic franchise model. Though Prajodh's franchising idea was initially questioned for its sustainability, his thorough research reinforced his confidence in his approach, eventually achieving remarkable success. This franchise model has a two-fold advantage:(a) support business expansion, and (b) promote entrepreneurship and employability, particularly among women.

'If you ask me, did we meet with resistance when we started? I would say otherwise, as we met with high demand, and we actually struggled to meet that demand. I remember once in Hyderabad in 2002, we decided to have one franchise seminar for the EuroKids concept. My expectation was that I would meet, at maximum ten potential franchise partners but to my surprise the room had around 100 people, majority of them were women who were eager to partner with us in our novel concept.'

Starting a EuroKids preschool franchise in any part of the country required an investment of around Rs 15 lakhs to Rs 20 lakhs, covering the franchise fee, infrastructure setup, furnishings, learning materials, and safety equipment. In addition, franchisees needed working capital to take care of operational expenses such as staff salaries, marketing, and maintenance. To turn this vision into reality, Prajodh realized a structured and supportive franchise model would be the key.

Prajodh emphasizes that EuroKids is not just a name lender, which led to the creation of a high-touch franchise owned and franchise operated model. To offer end-to-end support, the company has established a comprehensive franchise support program called EDGE360. It includes guidance on creating safe, child-friendly environments, access to research-backed curriculum, regular teacher training programs, marketing and operational support, and offering digital management and business tools for consistent smooth operations.

It's important to note that over 95 per cent of franchise owners are women, who have successfully transitioned from various professional backgrounds into entrepreneurship.

To facilitate their ownership, EuroKids, under the meticulous guidance and supervision of Prajodh and his team, offers collateral-free loans through its partnership with financial institutions at attractive interest rates for women. This initiative has not only promoted community development and self-reliance, especially among women but has also boosted employability.

Talking about the advantages of this model, Prajodh also elaborates on how they witnessed the incredible growth of EuroKids. While the publishing line of business initially helped support the launch of EuroKids, Prajodh explains that while the majority of the capital was bootstrapped, the rest was financed through institutional loans. Remarkably, within eighteen to twenty-four months, their franchise model propelled them from zero to 100 schools. By 2008, the network had grown to about 500, and by 2014, it had crossed 1,000 centres. Though the pandemic caused a temporary decline, the network has since returned to a strong and steady growth path.

What began as a strategic vision to establish the EuroKids network across 100 cities has evolved into a massive pan-India footprint, now spanning over 500+ cities. This expansion demonstrates a remarkable depth of reach, successfully bridging the gap between major metros and Tier 1 hubs to the heartlands of Tier 2 and Tier 3 towns. By scaling through such thoughtfully curated network, Prajodh has ensured that high-quality, 'Child First' early education is no longer reserved for the urban elite, but an accessible reality for families across the length and breadth of the nation.

To date, Prajodh and his team has established a network of 1,850+ preschools, with clear plans to surpass the 2,000 mark by next year. This remarkable scale underscores how the EuroKids franchise model has positioned the brand as the preeminent leader in the preschool sector, setting a benchmark for quality and operational excellence that remains the gold standard in a rapidly growing market.

BEYOND EUROKIDS: EXTENDING THE PROMISE OF LEARNING—FROM EARLY YEARS TO K-12

Under Prajodh's steady and purposeful leadership, EuroKids evolved into Lighthouse Learning Group, today a network of over 1,850 preschools and sixty schools across India, with a growing presence in international markets such as the Maldives, Qatar, and Nepal.

Building on the success of EuroKids, many franchise partners and parents encouraged Prajodh to explore the K-12 segment, prompting him to evaluate the possibilities. This led to the launch of EuroSchool in 2009, an extension of EuroKids. However, they decided against implementing the franchise model in the K-12 space, both because the ideal partner profile was unclear and because they wanted to meaningfully strengthen the K-12 system without transferring the ongoing responsibility of quality assurance and outcomes onto franchisees. They started with Mumbai, as both Prajodh and Vikas lived there, and in the very first year, the school enrolled around 297 students from kindergarten to grade 4.

Even for EuroSchool, Prajodh ensured that they didn't rely on standard publisher books. Instead, a dedicated central education team meticulously championed a **'Balanced Schooling'** philosophy—a holistic framework that blends foundational knowledge with 21st century skills, creating a dynamic environment where students develop the creativity and leadership necessary to thrive in the modern world.

The twenty-first EuroSchool is on its way, and what makes its arrival truly meaningful is the response it has already stirred. Even before the admissions office opened, several families gathered at the doorstep, eager to enrol their children. Their quiet anticipation spoke volumes—a genuine testament to the trust and confidence parents continue to place in the EuroSchool philosophy.

While EuroKids and EuroSchool cater to the preschool and K-12 segments with quality and affordable education, Prajodh's acquisition of Kangaroo kids, another preschool chain, and its K-12 extension Billabong High International School, was aimed at addressing the needs of Indians seeking more premium educational experiences. While the acquisition of Billabong High allowed Prajodh to evaluate the scalability of the franchise model in the K-12 sector, he decided to focus the growth strategy on a hybrid approach: continuing to successfully support the existing franchise partners along with prioritizing new self-owned schools in newer geographies to more closely align with their long-term vision.

Presently, the Lighthouse Learning network includes multiple educational brands including, EuroKids, EuroSchool, Kangaroo Kids, Billabong High International Schools, Centre Point Group of Schools, Heritage Xperiential Learning Schools, Phoenix Greens School of Learning and Finland International School Maldives with each one designed to meet diverse needs of students of different age groups. Lighthouse Learning is not a collection of brands—it is a shared belief system expressed in different forms. This network is driven by a singular vision of Lighthouse Learning: ***'To be the trusted choice for exceptional education in every community we serve.'***

To further accelerate the growth of the K-12 vertical, Prajodh focused on building a robust foundation of both financial and human capital. In 2013, he secured investment from Gaja Capital and Partners Group, a move that provided the financial resources necessary to significantly strengthen EuroSchool's footprint across the Indian education landscape. Beyond capital, Prajodh recognized that achieving a transformative vision required a diverse and powerhouse team; consequently, he attracted top-tier talent from across various industries. These professionals were drawn to the compelling vision and purpose of Lighthouse Learning, bringing cross-sector expertise to the mission of delivering world-class education at scale.

This balanced ecosystem of high-quality and international standard education offerings found powerful backing in 2019, when global investment firm KKR acquired a majority stake in EuroKids International. This partnership not only marked one of the largest private equity investments in India's education sector but also enabled Prajodh to widen their product offerings, strengthen his team, expand the network through acquisitions, and position Lighthouse Learning as a high-quality provider for early years and K-12 education in the country.

FROM VISION TO A MOVEMENT: HOW ONE ECOSYSTEM TRANSFORMED EDUCATION IN INDIA

'When I look back at these twenty-five years, I am grateful for the choice to anchor my life's work in India and its extraordinary potential. My aspiration has always been to scale with true impact – to ignite a lifelong love for learning in one million children, providing the foundation they need to grow, thrive, and build meaningful futures they deserve.'

Prajodh Rajan's journey is a testament to how one man's determination can transform an entire system. In India, pre-school was once viewed as a prelude to schooling, a place where children were taught to sit still, follow instructions, and prepare for the 'real' learning that awaited them in primary school. It was a scattered education system, where learning meant children memorizing alphabets and numbers, with little attention to the why's and how's behind them. Besides, emotional and personal development were often overlooked as foundations essential for later years as well, depriving children of the joy of nurturing their curiosity.

But Prajodh, through EuroKids and the thoughtfully sequenced expansion into EuroSchool and other chains, introduced much-needed structure to learning spaces, creating environments where children's imagination could run free and guide their learning. To this day, these spaces rest on pillars of uncompromising safety, reinforced by a technology-forward approach and guided by a child-centred curriculum designed not to dictate but to nurture young minds. Under his leadership, Lighthouse Learning has received several accolades, including titles such as 'Best Education Company', and 'India's Most Trusted Brand'. Further solidifying this legacy of excellence, the group has been recognized among 'India's Best Workplaces' in the Education and Training industry, and has earned the 'Great Place to Work' certification for the third consecutive year. These recognitions reflect his unwavering dedication to transforming the education landscape of India, and building a brand dedicated to nurturing a future-ready workforce that will drive the nation forward in every way possible.

For Prajodh, it has come full circle, from growing up watching teachers in his family excel in their field to creating opportunities for women to become education entrepreneurs and educators who can redefine the education landscape of India.

Looking ahead, Prajodh envisions extending his philosophy beyond K-12 education. His motto 'PG to PG' (Playgroup to Post Graduation) reflects his ambition to build a holistic learning ecosystem that supports individuals at every stage of their academic and professional journey, nurturing not just students, but lifelong learners ready to build meaningful and rewarding careers.

Prajodh believes that impact in Education is rarely instant and never individual. Real change happens when institutions are built patiently, values are protected fiercely, and people are placed at the centre of every decision. His commitment has always been to India—to its children, its educators, and its extraordinary potential. He believes that when education is done right, it does more than prepare students for exams or careers; it prepares them for life.

As Lighthouse Learning continues to evolve, Prajodh feels less like that of a founder and more like that of a custodian, ensuring that they never lose sight of why they began. If the next generation of learners grows up curious, confident, and compassionate, then every step of this journey would have been worth it.

'When I reflect on this journey, I don't see milestones or numbers as much as I see people—teachers who chose this profession as a calling, parents who trusted us with their children, partners who believed in our long-term vision, and teams who work tirelessly behind the scenes to redefine the classroom experience, making learning more meaningful, inclusive, safer and attuned to the needs of the learner.'

SECTION 2

Changing Outcomes

The road of education leads to different outcomes. For some, it's the path to a well-defined job, often through a maze of competitive tests, each tougher than the other. For others, it's the confidence that we can keep adapting as our lives evolve. For an even fewer and select group of people, it's the absolute joy of learning, not just during the years of school and college, but the constant act of learning as a lifelong skill.

Meet the visionaries who have made such a powerful education impact real, from making access easier to quality deeper to redefining what lifelong learning can meet in today's age of AI led shifts in jobs and work.

CHAPTER 4

From Reel to Real—Pathways to Lifelong Learning

Ronnie Screwvala, Founder of UTV and upGrad

'For him, growth was an everyday manifestation.'

EARLY LIFE AND THE SEEDS OF SELF-BELIEF

In the crowded lanes of Mumbai, before the skyscrapers rose and the city began to run on the adrenaline of global finance, a boy named Ronnie grew up in a modest flat. His world was small but vivid, the hum of ceiling fans in the summer heat, the clang of steel lunch tiffin packed every morning, the scratch of chalk on classroom blackboards. He was not born into wealth or legacy.

'***I would say lower middle-class background,'*** Ronnie recalls matter-of-factly, ***'and therefore, I think it triggered me to actually go out and say I want to be an entrepreneur … I would say no. A, because no reservoir of funding. B,***

no family business. C, no family track record of being in entrepreneurship. D, therefore, obviously at risk from a personal financial point of view.'

His father was a career professional, working across multiple Tata companies before moving into a multinational. His brother took the academic route, earning a PhD in HR and building a career in global banking. In a family that valued stability, the idea of stepping into the unknown, starting something of your own, wasn't just unusual, it was almost unthinkable.

But young Ronnie was already being shaped by forces that didn't fit into report cards or career counselling. His school years were split between two very different worlds. Until the seventh standard, he attended a grounded, middle-class school named Dunn's Institute. Then, in the eighth, a sudden shift occurred: he moved to Cathedral in the eighth standard. The Cathedral and John Connon School was one of Mumbai's most prestigious schools, a place where the children of industrialists and professionals arrived in chauffeur-driven cars and left for homes that felt like palaces compared to Ronnie's modest apartment.

The contrast was stark. He remembers how he would carry lunch every day from home while others would enjoy their warm lunch sitting in their car, delivered from home each day.

For some, such an observation might have bred insecurity or resentment. For Ronnie, it became a source of confidence. At Cathedral, he found himself among peers who would one day inherit family businesses and political legacies. His best friend at the time, Rohinton Nariman, was the son of Fali Nariman, one of India's most respected jurists.

Despite knowing that almost 60 per cent of his friends were people who were going to walk into their family business at some stage or the other, he did not feel rattled or intimidated by it. Instead, it planted a seed of awareness of another world. The exposure wasn't just about wealth; it was about conversations at dinner tables, about ambition spoken of as a birthright instead of a gamble.

But academics didn't stir his soul, something else did. *Theatre.* Standing under the stage lights, feeling the hum of an audience before the first line was spoken, he discovered a form of confidence no exam could offer.

Theatre wasn't just performance; it was discipline, collaboration, and resourcefulness. It was producing a play with limited means, learning to ask for sponsorships, meeting advertising executives in glass-walled offices, convincing them to invest in an idea. He performed his hobbies.

It was also, unknowingly, the start of his entrepreneurial education.

THE SETBACK THAT BECAME A CATALYST

By the time Ronnie reached college, the momentum from Cathedral and theatre carried him forward but not necessarily towards textbooks. He enrolled in a commerce program, a choice that felt less like ambition and more like the path of least resistance.

However, soon came a massive shock. Ronnie failed in his second year in college.

'That was the door closing. everything else felt "hum, ha, hoo." It was a huge shock. Huge setback. Huge failure.'

In a city where academic progression was seen as a linear climb toward stability, failing a year was more than a delay; it was a public stumble. The mechanics of the failure were almost worse than the event itself. He had to keep studying the same subjects for four months, skip college, appear for an exam midterm, sort of catch up, and above all, lose an entire year.

But unlike some who might have rationalized the failure away as a mismatch of ability, Ronnie knew the cause: He knew it wasn't a reaction that 'Oh see, I'm not made for studies because I failed', he knew exactly why he had failed—overconfidence and swagger.

In that enforced pause something shifted. The failure didn't push him toward redemption through academia; it pushed him towards an alternative. By then, his extracurricular life was rich enough to offer options. He was producing plays, doing voice work, and even earning money. He received his first check when he did a voice recording for a Cadbury's commercial with O&M during the first year of his college.

That voice work wasn't luck, it was the direct result of his theatre hustle. He used to meet agencies to acquire sponsorships, meet the creative directors, accounts directors, and that's how one thing connected to another, and one day, somebody decided to check his voice since his diction sounded good.

The Cadbury's ad led to more voiceovers, comparing shows, and eventually producing theatre at a larger scale. That financial independence, modest as it was, gave him something rare for someone his age—the freedom to take risks and produce theatre.

Still, at home, there was unease. His brother's path had been clear and academic; Ronnie's was unconventional and uncertain.

'I don't think they were comfortable but they were not unsupportive. They were obviously stressed about it and I'd already put them through a lot of stress by failing in my second year in college anyway. So I don't think there could be more stress than that.'

It was a turning point, the moment when the 'safe' door to an academic and corporate future closed, and the only one left was the one he'd have to build himself.

THE FIRST VENTURES—CABLE TV AND TOOTHBRUSHES

When most people look back at their first jobs, they think of cubicles, ID cards, and monthly salaries. For Ronnie, it was three months at an advertising agency—'just calling the pub,' as he puts it. It didn't last.

Instead, his first real venture was something entirely different—cable television. It was the early 1980s, and television in India was still a monopoly. Doordarshan was the only channel, and the idea of having multiple options, let alone niche programming, seemed like a fantasy. But in pockets of the country, small entrepreneurs were finding ways to beam alternative programming directly into homes via cable networks.

Ronnie saw the opening and, more importantly, believed he could fill it. The business was hands-on. It meant installing equipment in people's homes, running cables across streets and buildings, curating content that would actually draw viewers away from the national broadcaster. It also meant operating in a legal grey area. The Copyright Act was not clear, individuals were operating under the Post and Telegraphs Act, but it was ultimately only the government that could cross cables across municipal roads.

From the start, it was a balancing act—one part creativity, one part technical, and one part navigating bureaucracy. The success gave him confidence, but it also gave him cash flow to think bigger.

Around the same time, another opportunity arrived, one far less glamorous, but surprisingly stable: toothbrush manufacturing. It was a business rooted in the small-scale industry sector, where large companies like Colgate couldn't manufacture their own products directly.

'It was purely a contract manufacturing business,' Ronnie explains. ***'Once you sign contracts with large manufacturers, large brands, you are good to capitalize. Solid technology from Belgium and China was available at that point in time.'***

If cable TV was a creative gamble, toothbrush manufacturing was a steady march. It was about machinery, contracts, and consistent output. To him, it did offer much more stable income, revenue, and profitability; basically, a decent cash flow to fund some of the things that had more up and down, like cable TV.

His empathy for small-scale entrepreneurs of today comes directly from those years. It wasn't easy. The industry had its own politics, its own funding challenges, and its own bottlenecks. But compared to the unpredictability of the media, it was, as Ronnie says, ***'more sensible, more tangible, real, that you can build out.'***

Running both ventures in parallel taught him a crucial lesson: diversification was not just a buzzword, it was survival. The stability of manufacturing gave him room to push boundaries in the media. The creative energy of cable TV kept him from getting complacent in manufacturing.

Eventually, he sold the cable TV business, ironically to the very COO he had hired. The sale wasn't emotional. For Ronnie, it was about pragmatism, something he would carry into every future exit, whether in media or education.

As he puts it: ***'There is always a cost in which you can operate and still be above the water even in the worst of times but for that, you have to build for it, and you have to have a sense that you don't have any other choice but to stay afloat.'***

THE BIRTH OF UTV—FROM STAGE TO SCREEN

By the early 1990s, Ronnie had two businesses running—cable TV for creativity, toothbrush manufacturing for stability. But the gravitational pull of storytelling, of the stage and screen, was still strong.

Then came the phone call that would change the course of his career.

It was from Alyque Padamsee—the iconic adman and theatre personality with whom Ronnie had performed on stage. Alyque was then the head of Lintas, one of India's biggest advertising agencies. Lintas had a client, Thomson Associates, who wanted to commission a television-sponsored show.

It was an opportunity, but also a leap into the unknown. Producing television content was a different animal from theatre. Sets had to be built for the camera, scripts had to be tight, schedules were relentless. But Ronnie's instinct was to say yes first and figure out the rest.

He pulled in people he trusted from the theatre circuit. He recalls how they had all connected through stage work. One of them, his eventual co-founder, was creating ad commercials at the time. That's when he suggested they join forces and build something together.

There was also Zarina, now his wife, but then just a friend from the stage. She was doing theatre, so she came in, and Ronnie got her into post-production and editing on that first show that Alyque had done.

The momentum built quickly. That first show led to more—corporate videos, commercials, documentaries. Then came the call from Procter & Gamble, via yet another theatre connection.

'***P&G used to sponsor a lot of theatre, so Gulcharan Das, at that stage, wanted to do a daily soap opera. Because P&G worldwide was doing daily soap operas. So, he reached out to Madison's Sam Balsara and said, "We've got to find somebody." Then they came back to me and said, "Will you do India's first daily soap opera?" We had no clue how to do it. But that's what we did. We did Shanti.***'

Shanti was a gamble. Daily soaps didn't exist in India then. The production schedule was punishing—scripts written on the fly, episodes shot and edited at breakneck pace to meet telecast deadlines. But it worked. The show became a phenomenon, cementing UTV's reputation in television.

If theatre had been the training ground, *Shanti* was the proving ground. The show taught Ronnie that success wasn't about waiting until you were ready, it was about being willing to take the plunge before you thought you were ready.

Interestingly, Ronnie doesn't frame these opportunities as 'networking wins.' In fact, he rejects the word entirely. He doesn't see himself as quintessentially a networking guy at all. Mostly, people around him saw his calibre and reached out to him with some incredible opportunities.

For him, theatre wasn't a strategic stepping stone to television, it was simply a passion. But the relationships built there, the trust earned, and the work ethic displayed had opened doors in unexpected ways.

And just like that, UTV, which started as a small group of theatre friends taking on a sponsored show, was becoming a full-fledged media production company. The stage lights were giving way to camera lights. The audience was growing from a few hundred in an auditorium to millions in living rooms across India.

The next step? Scaling from television into films, gaming, and beyond and eventually, preparing for the boldest move yet: taking UTV public and later selling to Disney.

SCALING THE DREAM—UTV TO DISNEY

With *Shanti*, a household name, UTV's credibility solidified, and Ronnie faced a choice: stay comfortable in television or push into bigger, riskier territory.

Comfort, he decided, was overrated.

UTV began to diversify aggressively. It expanded into more television programming, corporate videos, animation, gaming, and eventually films. Each move meant learning an entirely new business from scratch. He was well aware that not everything would work in terms of timing. Between the first contract and the next, opening factories in five states took a fair bit of time. At that stage, one could have lost oneself. But he stayed the course.

That phrase, *stay the course*, is a Ronnie Screwvala signature. For him, scaling wasn't about reckless expansion; it was about persistence in the face of uncertainty, tempered with a willingness to pivot when necessary.

The film business brought a different scale of ambition. Budgets were bigger, risks higher, timelines longer. The stakes went beyond programming slots into box-office returns and international distribution. Yet the DNA of UTV's early days of resourcefulness, creative instinct, and relentless execution carried over.

By the mid-2000s, UTV was one of India's most recognized media houses. But Ronnie was already thinking ahead.

'I don't think anyone sets out with a goal ... that you set out to build multiple businesses,' he says. ***'That's a little mythical. You build one, and then another opportunity comes along, and you take it.'***

The ultimate opportunity came from The Walt Disney Company. They were looking to deepen their footprint in India and saw UTV as the perfect partner. For Ronnie, it wasn't just about the payday but about aligning with a global giant that could take the company further than he could alone.

The negotiations were long, the due diligence exhaustive. But when the deal closed in 2012, it was historic: Disney acquired UTV for an enterprise value of then $1.4 billion dollars, taking full control and marking one of the largest deals in Indian media history.

'There is always a cost in which you can operate and still be above the water even in the worst of times but for that, you have to build for it. You have to have a sense that you don't have any other choice but to stay afloat.'

In other words, exits are part of the game. If the conditions are right, you take them, not because you've fallen out of love with what you've built but because the move creates space for the next big thing.

For Ronnie, that 'next big thing' was already forming in his mind. He had experienced media, manufacturing, and entertainment at scale. Now, he was ready to turn his attention to something even more transformative: Education.

THE EDUCATION BET—FOUNDING UPGRAD

The ink on the Disney deal was barely dry when Ronnie began asking himself a deceptively simple question: ***'If I'm going to build something again, will it be just profitable . . . or will it truly matter?'***

He had spent decades in the media, influencing pop culture, telling stories, shaping narratives. But now he wanted to shape something even more fundamental: lives. In his view, nothing had a deeper, longer-lasting impact than education.

Spotting the Gap

By 2014, the Indian education landscape was brimming with promise but was also riddled with gaps. Universities were churning out graduates who weren't job ready. Professionals were desperate to upskill but found traditional courses outdated, inaccessible, or both.

Ronnie saw the same pattern he had spotted in the media years ago: a sector ripe for disruption, stuck in an old operating system. Technology could close the gap but only if it was paired with industry relevance and a strong learner experience.

He recalls, ***'In the media, I always believed in direct-to-consumer. Why should education be any different? Why can't we give professionals direct access to world-class learning, without making them leave their jobs or cities?'***

The vision crystallized: an online education platform focused on upskilling working professionals in emerging industries—data science, AI, management, and entrepreneurship.

The Founding

In early 2015, Ronnie co-founded upGrad with Mayank Kumar, Phalgun Kompalli, and Ravijot Chugh. The mission was clear: not to be a "content dump" platform, but to deliver structured, high-quality programs with measurable outcomes.

'I didn't want to just make videos and call it education,' he says. ***'The learner has to feel guided. There has to be mentorship, industry projects, peer-to-peer learning. Otherwise, it's just passive consumption and that doesn't change careers.'***

The team started small with a handful of employees, one modest office, and a few pilot programs. But the ambition was anything but modest.

They partnered with top universities like IIIT-Bangalore, O.P Jindal Global University and MICA to create rigorous, recognized programs. They embedded career support into the model, from interview prep to placement assistance. They invested heavily in learner engagement, with live sessions, mentors, and interactive projects.

Early Scepticism

The first months were filled with doubts–many from within. Ronnie realised that online education was still an untested concept in India. People around him dismissed his ideas as unrealistic, and that made him question if professionals would truly be willing to do a six-month or one-year program online.

But the early batches proved his thesis. Completion rates were high, learner satisfaction strong, and most importantly, graduates were landing better jobs. Word spread, enrolments grew, and upGrad began scaling at a pace that surprised even its founders.

Philosophy of Scale

For Ronnie, scaling upGrad wasn't just about marketing spend or rapid course launches. It was about trust. ***'Education is one of the few businesses where your brand is built entirely on outcomes,'*** he says. ***'If you overpromise and underdeliver, you're done.'***

This meant saying no to easy wins, like shallow celebrity-taught "courses" that generated buzz but little real value. ***'We were clear that*** **if we put something out there, it has to change someone's life in a tangible way.'**

By 2021, upGrad had expanded into multiple categories—from partner-led certifications to university-led degrees to study abroad pathways; a full-stack learning ecosystem for anyone over eighteen years of age to sixty and above, and had served learners in over 100 countries. Investors valued it at over $2 billion, making it one of India's few promising unicorns in edtech, which today has matured into a global skilling major emerging out of India.

Why Education?

When asked why he chose education after such a successful media career, Ronnie's answer is both pragmatic and philosophical:

'I've done entertainment. I've done manufacturing. I've done media. But if I'm going to spend the next twenty years building something, I want it to be in a sector that transforms people, not just entertains them. Education gives you that. It's impact at scale.'

For Ronnie, upGrad wasn't just a business. It's a culmination of his belief in lifelong learning, his experience building consumer brands, and his conviction that the next great Indian companies will be built on human capital.

And in his mind, he was just getting started.

LESSONS FROM THE JOURNEY

When Ronnie Screwvala talks about entrepreneurship, he does so without the halo effect of hindsight. There's no glossy rewriting of the past, no airbrushed victories. His stories are full of near-misses, pivots, and recoveries, and the kind of details that don't make it into most press releases.

That is exactly why his lessons resonate.

1. Serendipity Over Script

Ronnie is quick to dismiss the idea of a preordained career path. ***'Dots to dots connect but they are not factual, pre-planned. Normally, dots don't get connected when you have a path. Dots get connected where it happens serendipitously.'***

It's a perspective born from a career that has zigzagged between theatre, cable TV, toothbrush manufacturing, media, and edtech. For him, opportunity often comes disguised as something else entirely—a hobby, a side gig, a casual introduction.

The key, he insists, is to be alert to these moments, even if they don't fit your "plan."

2. Self-Confidence is Built, Not Born

Ronnie's belief in his own ability to take risks didn't spring fully formed. It was cultivated in small stages—acting in plays, hosting shows, producing theatre. This is why he encourages young entrepreneurs to push themselves into unfamiliar situations; not for the sake of discomfort, but because confidence grows when you succeed in contexts where you weren't sure you could.

3. Risk Without Recklessness

Despite his adventurous career, Ronnie rejects the idea that entrepreneurs must be natural risk-takers. He reminds how in his own journey there was no reservoir of funding, no family business, no entrepreneurial track record.

He argues that true entrepreneurial risk is calculated, you make the leap only when you believe you can land. When you do, you find ways to stay afloat no matter what.

4. The Power of Staying the Course

Ronnie's ventures have rarely been overnight successes. Whether it was growing UTV into a media powerhouse or establishing upGrad as a global edtech brand, the pattern is the same—slow build, constant iteration, eventual scale. In his view, most entrepreneurs quit too early. They mistake a temporary stall for a permanent wall.

5. Environment Shapes Ambition

Ronnie credits much of his early self-awareness to being exposed to peers from vastly different backgrounds after moving to Cathedral school. For him, the takeaway is clear: if your environment isn't stretching your perspective, you have to find ways to change it physically, socially, or intellectually.

6. Outcomes Build Trust

In education, Ronnie is adamant that marketing can only get you so far. The real brand is built in the results your learners achieve. He firmly believes that education is one of the few businesses where your brand is built entirely on outcomes. If you overpromise and underdeliver, you're done.

This same principle applies across industries according to him. Deliver consistently, and trust compounds over time. Break it once, and it's almost impossible to rebuild.

7. Pragmatism Over Attachment

Perhaps one of Ronnie's most unromantic but most valuable lessons is the importance of knowing when to exit. Whether selling the cable business to his COO or UTV to Disney, he approaches each decision with detachment.

'Exits are part of the game. If the conditions are right, you take them. Not because you've fallen out of love with what you've built, but because the move creates space for the next big thing.'

This mindset allows him to avoid the trap of over-identifying with a single venture. The company is the mission, not the identity.

8. The Long View

Ronnie's career arc shows a clear pattern, he doesn't chase quick wins. Even his current venture, upGrad, is positioned for a twenty-year horizon. It's a philosophy that rejects the glamour of "serial entrepreneurship" for the discipline of building enduring institutions.

FULL CIRCLE, OR PERHAPS THE NEXT BIG THING

When Ronnie Screwvala looks back at the arc of his life, he doesn't see a perfectly plotted map. He sees a winding road, full of unmarked turns, detours, and moments that could easily have gone another way. Yet, each twist added something—a skill, a connection, a conviction—that made the next leap possible.

From the outside, it might look like he leapt from one high-stakes industry to another with fearless confidence. But in his telling, the story is more grounded: one decision at a time, each based on what was in front of him, each shaped by the same core principles.

What ties theatre, cable TV, toothbrush manufacturing, UTV, and upGrad together isn't the sector. It's a mindset of "something more" that kept evolving. In the early days, it was about survival—making ends meet through voiceovers, sponsorship deals, small productions. Later, it became about scale—growing UTV into one of India's largest media houses. Today, it's about impact—using upGrad to give millions of learners' access to skills and opportunities.

However, whenever a venture reached a point where someone else could take it further, he let it go. Whenever an opportunity looked unfamiliar but promising, he stepped in anyway.

With upGrad, he's betting on the idea that the most valuable currency of the future won't be content or entertainment, it will be skills. He wants to build the bridge that helps people cross from where they are to where they could be.

That said, Ronnie doesn't see upGrad as his "final" act, but he does see it as the one with the longest runway. The media was fast, volatile, and often dependent on trends. Education, he believes, will only grow in relevance.

In some ways, Ronnie's story has come full circle. The boy who once saw theatre as a hobby now sees education as a calling. The entrepreneur who once sold UTV to Disney now mentors and backs new founders. The man who once built entertainment empires now builds platforms for learning.

The 'next big thing', for Ronnie Screwvala, isn't a mystery. It's already here, growing one learner at a time.

CHAPTER 5

Education Equity—A Dream Made Real

Shaheen Mistri, Founder of 'Teach for India'

'She saw possibility in every child, power in every teacher.'

EARLY INFLUENCES—PEOPLE AND PLACES WHO HELPED IN THE MAKING OF A CHANGEMAKER

In India, education inequity has long been a battle many failed to acknowledge let alone conquer. However, in 2009, one radical visionary, Shaheen Mistri, the founder of Teach for India, a globally renowned non-profit organization set her mind to make education equally accessible to every child in India, irrespective of their gender, geographical location, and social background.

It is true that one's early life experiences play a pivotal role in defining their thought process. It was the same for Mistri. Though a part of a relatively big Parsi family, she was closer to her nuclear family as she lived away from India during her formative years. Her parents significantly contributed to inculcating the right set of values and pushing her to explore her potential from a very young age.

'When I was ten years old, my father bought a very beautiful piano, and I wasn't that interested in playing it. But you know, every day, I was told "you have to play piano for two to three hours a day." He embodied being extremely productive. Sunday Mornings, my brother and I would get up by 9:30 a.m. but our father would have already checked off three things of his daily chore list.'

Her father, a banker, taught her to have high standards, be disciplined and organized, and stay consistently productive. Her mother, a speech therapist, often worked with children with various special needs and brought a sense of warmth to every space she entered.

Mistri and her mother share a creative streak, and they have co-authored several children's books, later titled '*Miss Mugli*', and travelled extensively.

Mistri's role model was her maternal grandmother, a free-spirited highly creative individual. She deeply inspired how Mistri led her own life.

'My nani would cut down her curtains when she got tired of them and make them into clothes to wear. She started painting at the age of seventy and was sure she could teach herself. Didn't want to waste money even though she had enough. Instead of investing in paper or canvas for her art, she would use medical calendars gifted by my grandfather

as the canvas. She was a real-free spirit. Never cared what anyone thought of her. She was extremely creative; would write poems, record cassettes, and tell us scary stories. She was just very special. She had a love marriage, which was unusual during those times and would show us the love letters.'

Volunteering also played an indispensable part in Mistri's childhood, preparing her for a future deeply rooted in the Indian social sector.

'***So, from the age of twelve, I spent every summer volunteering in India. I worked at the happy home and school for the blind. I worked in the Education Audiology and Research Center, setup by my mother, for the hearing impaired. In New York, I spent a summer volunteering with autistic children. In Indonesia, I worked with an orphanage that had a room with children who were very unwell. So, these were extremely formative experiences for me.***'

THE MOMENT, THE 'WHY' TOOK ROOT—AWAKENING OF A PURPOSE WITH THE AKANKSHA FOUNDATION

From a very young age, Mistri became aware of the privileges she had. Whether it was the freedom to visit her grandparents in India, access to high-quality education, or the opportunity to volunteer in the social sector from early teenage years she recognized her encounters with disparity. Even to those young eyes, the world didn't seem fair or equal toward everyone, and that awareness often stirred a sense of guilt in her. It pushed her to ask relevant questions and take meaningful steps towards bridging social inequalities that she saw around her.

'To me, it just seemed like an element of chance that was the underpinning of privilege. I questioned why I had the opportunities I did, and why others didn't. I think that question carried a lot of guilt until I returned to India and did something about it.'

While her entire childhood contributed to the belief that she had to break the conventional shackles preventing children from unprivileged backgrounds from accessing education, a defining moment pushed her to return to India. At the age of eighteen, while studying at Tufts University in the United States, she was visiting Mumbai for a vacation. She was sitting in a taxi waiting for the traffic light to turn green, when a few kids ran to the car to beg for money and food. Instead of brushing them off, she engaged in a conversation with them instead. It was then that a girl expressed her desire to go to school like others but simply didn't have the means to.

That brief encounter turned out to be the life-altering moment that shook Mistri to the core, cementing the importance of education. Following that interaction, Shaheen visited various shelters and slums to get a deeper understanding of what the underprivileged kids were going through. To bring her vision to life of making education more accessible, Mistri dropped out of Tufts and joined St. Xavier's College in Mumbai.

However, just a few days into her college, she was left stunned. No one took studies seriously. The way of learning felt completely different from what she was used to. In the U.S, students were pushed to think and debate, whereas here, she could see everyone becoming passive recipients of learning. Instead of delving deep into the topics, many would purchase textbooks close to the exams, memorize everything and somehow manage to get through.

Wanting to immerse herself in the country after the years of disconnect, she sought out internships and volunteering gigs. After a short informal internship stint under a journalist and volunteering at the Social Service League at Xavier's, she decided to go into the community directly and teach. It was during this time that she realized three things: (1) There were a lot of college students spending their ideal time sipping cups of coffee, (2) there was plenty space in the city that could be used, and (3) a lot of young children expressed the eagerness to learn. This eventually led her to envision Akanksha—a non-profit organization started by her in 1991, which focused on offering premium-quality education to children from low-income families.

However, bringing her vision to life was not easy as finding the volunteers was a tedious job.

'I think I did very random things. I hand painted posters saying you can make a difference. Spent a lot of time in the canteen talking to people. Goading fellow classmates to contribute to make the country better by volunteering to teach.'

Along with finding ways to convince people around her to volunteer, Mistri spent a great deal of time in the community to closely observe and understand the struggles of low-income families. This immersion further solidified her decision to start Akanksha. Witnessing both their hardships and resilience, and the rich sense of community they harboured regardless, reminded of the privileges she had lived her childhood with and how eagerly she wanted them to experience the same.

During the earlier days at Akanksha, Mistri made a conscious decision to immerse herself deep into the lives of the children she was teaching. She wanted to understand what they liked, how they wanted to be taught, the need of their families, and how those needs affected their participation in school. She became an active learner herself. From raising funds to getting best equipment for Montessori teaching technique and personally visiting families to find out why practices like corporal punishment were normalized and prevalent in the community.

She offered sewing lessons to older girls to help them earn money while studying, and taught mothers how to fold paper bags as a means of livelihood. She took it upon herself to do whatever it took to prevent children from dropping out of their program. She collaborated with hospitals to ensure her students and their families lived healthier and more informed lives.

While Akanksha was earlier an after-school initiative, Mistri started recognizing the gaps in learning that prompted her to transition it into a full-fledged school model. For instance, at Akanksha, kids were taught to consider it a safe space and express their voices and opinions, which was something not preferred in the government schools. Hence, five years into Akanksha, she felt more confident and less daunting in taking over the schools.

'Every day there would be kids who were not enrolled in Akanksha waiting to get onto that bus, and they would literally run behind the bus, including going as far as hanging off its back. And so, for me, scale was a response to that. I said, "how do we do it for more kids?" So that was the impetus and the intention to scale.'

Mistri knew that expanding her vision required a series of strategic moves, supported by honest trial and error. One day, an interaction with a young girl 'Rachna' sparked an idea: support volunteers by hiring teachers for scaling Akanksha's school model. Rachna asked Mistri why they didn't include paid teachers, pointing out that relying solely on volunteers came with drawbacks, the lack of commitment from the volunteers to be a major one. That is how they got their first teacher, and soon after, decided to register Akanksha as an organization in order to raise funds to support the growing needs of the school and its children.

Once three-four Akanksha centres were up and running, Mistri started putting in place simple documentation to help organizations replicate the model, leading to its widespread adoption.

'So, we said, let a unit be sixty kids which means we just need four volunteers and probably two paid teachers in

a centre on any given day. We visualized what the centre would look like. Around this time a friend told me that some organizations participate in sponsor-a-school-programs. That idea spoke to me, and I wondered why someone would not want to pay a couple of lakhs per year to run a whole centre.'

With this meticulous vision in mind, she started a 'sponsor a school' scheme. She would often carry details and pictures of Akanksha centres to successfully approach the potential sponsors. She would explain to them how they could adopt an agency and put their name on it, which led to an organic scaling of the Akanksha model, gradually turning into a replicable playbook that anyone could easily adopt.

Seeding of TFI (Teach for India)—From Offering Lessons to Planting Leaders

Akanksha Foundation took flight with Mistri's vision of high-quality education regardless of economic and social backgrounds. However, she saw that the real barrier in the country's education sector was not just infrastructure or curriculum, but effective leadership. She realized that to eliminate educational inequity at a national scale, the country needed thousands of young individuals who were passionate enough to drive change, something which the talent pipeline alone at Akanksha was incapable of doing. This led to the birth of TFI (Teach for India) initiative in the year 2009, eighteen years after she laid the foundation of the Akanksha initiative.

Mistri always found joy in being around children and working within the education landscape. Though starting TFI meant moving one level away from being in direct contact with children, TFI was estimated to enable a ripple effect. It offered a strategic path to drive systemic change through people who could have an outsized exponential impact on children over time. So, to turn this dream into a living reality, she introduced the two-year TFI Fellowship, a full-time program that places passionate young professionals and teachers in under-resourced schools across India.

'Seventeen years into Akanksha, we were just starting to see results of kids having completed college, getting jobs, bringing about real shifts in their families and their communities. It was a very fun time to be at Akanksha. For many years, I had asked myself what I want to be doing, but because of the children it changed to "Where do I need to have the most impact during TFI?"'

Mistri vividly remembers how enthusiastic, idealistic, and passionate the first cohort of TFI fellows was. It was filled with individuals who experienced a sense of pride in operating and being received as teachers. They were willing to try unconventional teaching methods to build deep and close relationships with students in order to get a proper understanding of the gaps they needed to address. Along with delivering lessons to students, these fellows were able to develop leadership, problem-solving, and engagement skills—qualities that TFI continues to cultivate in individuals committed to bringing a transformative change to India's education landscape.

Mistri understood the importance of not letting the essence of TFI sway away as they scaled and expanded.

'I have always said that practice and culture have always been two most important things to me. I focused on how to practice what I wanted to see in other people. I looked at how one can be open and transparent when they've not lived the culture, so that people could learn from the mistakes and grow.'

To ensure that the work culture remained consistent, Mistri moved the initial fellows to different parts of the organization, allowing the culture to grow around those who embodied it. In addition, she embedded it into the fabric of TFI's structure and processes, leaving no room for its disruptions. For fellows, the cultural foundation was laid right from the beginning of their journey at the training institute. For instance, if the fellows believed that student-teacher relationship was the most important thing, then their journey as a fellow started with forging that connection.

Additionally, TFI's ethos is further upheld with regular check-ins, performance appraisals, and day-to-day discussions with industry leaders. Doing so massively assisted in determining where the business philosophy was spreading and where it was breaking down.

However, Mistri faced three persistent challenges that were glaringly obvious to her from the first day of TFI's inception. To begin with, the individual lived realities of the children's low-income upbringing. Second has been funding; even with the brand lasting years, funding continues to be an everyday priority to ensure stability. The third challenge was curating the right team to take forward TFI's mission and vision.

Nonetheless, she believes that the leadership team of TFI has always held real responsibility for the legacy it wishes to leave behind. Additionally, the board has played a crucial role in mapping out day-to-day strategic governance and lending unconditional support.

'***Anu Aga chaired our board for the first decade and Nisa Godrej has now taken over the responsibility. Having a board that really engages with the real issues and asks difficult questions but is also available for the tiniest of things helps massively. For example, one of our TFI's students who got into a Law college asked me to help gather funds for a laptop. Within seven minutes of sending the request to the leadership team, we had raised the required amount for the fundraiser. So, this is something I feel very proud of.'***

Reflecting on the challenges associated with education equity that Mistri continues to experience second-hand and is working to eliminate, she says, ***'The most prevalent challenge continues to be making teaching aspirational for young minds. I believe many don't aspire this noble pursuit and on the rare occasions that they do, most aspirants get abysmal training required to become a teacher. I feel like the sector doesn't know how to invest in teachers nor value and support them.'***

Education today, she argues, has become too focused on individual achievement, instead of promoting empathetic and social achievements. This systematically has led to a capitalist persona which prioritizes material gains even if it's at the expense of social concerns like climate change. Hence, if the purpose of education is re-structured to go beyond one's own needs and career goals, it can begin to tackle these larger systemic issues.

'Growing up I used to believe that if I tick off a few silver bullet points, I could drive change. Now, I believe that the only way to change the education system is to have thousands of people doing small things.'

Mistri, an educationalist who was extremely angry at the systematic division of education, now believes love to be a much powerful force; slower, less visible but highly effective. A substantial shift in her personality has been influenced by her construct of collective leadership, allowing every individual a chance to lead.

To young entrepreneurs, her piece of advice is to have a balance between head and heart. While India's education system has trained our minds, it is important to follow our primal instincts, especially in a world drowning with overwhelming amounts of information. She suggests taking little steps every day, as it isn't important to know what you want to do in the next fifty years, but just what you wish to do tomorrow.

'Overcome your fear of taking the first step, and that step will lead to second, third, and fourth, and eventually build into a big crazy dream. That one little step may go backwards once in a while, and that's okay as well. I tell this to every cohort of fellows; be gentle to yourself. The work is hard, so cultivate that gentleness within yourself. I used to think that being gentle was being weak. I realized that being gentle actually gives you strength to work hard on yourself and drive change.'

CHAPTER 6

Democratizing Learning—Quality Education Brought Home

Ashwin Damera, Co-Founder of Eruditus and Emeritus

'He turned distance into connection and aspiration into access.'

CHALK DUST AND FOUNDATION LESSONS

Two decades ago, enrolling in a course offered by an Ivy league institution was a dream many aspired to but only a few privileged could turn into reality.

The high cost of premium quality education often prevented many bright minds from being nurtured in institutions with a long-standing legacy of transforming lives through world-class education and opening doors to success.

However, for one person and one company, that challenge was an invitation to solve, laying forth the foundation for a mission—make global quality education accessible. Meet

arwal Reflecting Her Career as a Long-Standing Civil Servant

arwal With Her Family Celebrating Daughter's Graduation

Karwal Exchanging Greetings With The Dalai Lama

Dhawan Exchanging Honours in a Gesture of Mutual Respect

Planting Seeds of Sustainability and Growth

Ashish Dhawan in Thoughtful Reflection at Ashoka University

Damera Capped and Gowned Before Harvard's Iconic Halls

Ashwin and Chaitanya - Founders of One of India's Leading India-Bred Global EdTech Companies

Ashwin and Chaitanya in Conversation at an Education Forum

Setting Foundation to Ryan Group With Fr. Agnelo High School

Guinness World Record Triumph with the Ryan Family

Grace Pinto in Dialogue with Prime Minister Narendra Modi

Chaudhry Cuts the Ribbon at an Aakash branch With Family By His Side

Roots of Resilience in Family Portrait

Multi-Generational Legacy at the Helm

Kiranbir Nurturing the "I Can" Mindset at Home

Echoes of Gandhi in Modern Pedagogy

Global Embrace for Humane Education

Prajodh at Inauguration of New Eurokids Campus

Young Prajodh Living With His Parents in Kerala

Prajodh With His Family in Festive Season

Laying the Foundation for ISB's Legacy

Convening Visionaries at Founding Day of Ashoka University

Inspiring Global Leaders from London Skies

'awar in The 1st Year of NIIT

'awar Working on a Computer in March 1981 – Early Days of NIIT

Pawar Conferred With The Padma Bhushan by The President in 2011

Pawar With Bhutan Ex PM, Mr Jigmi Y Thinley and India PM, Manmohan Singh

upGrad's Founding
Trio United

Hands-On Learning in Rural Classrooms

Ronnie Screwvala - The Visionary
in a Thoughtful Pose

Shaheen the storyteller

Community group on steps with Shaheen

Storytime in the School Library

Sunny Varkey Standing Tall in Reflective Grandeur

Ashwin Damera, Co-founder and CEO of Eruditus and Emeritus.

The roots of which took seed decades back in his carefree childhood days. Following his brother's footsteps, Damera got into KFI (Krishnamurti Foundation India) School, an unconventional institution built on the campus of Theosophical Society, just a short walk from their home at the time.

Reminiscing on his school days, Damera shares, ***'It changed my view on life and education in general. We had no uniforms, many classes were taught in the open with nature, no exams till 8th standard, no sense of competition. They wanted to express themselves and not be confined. For example, I started playing cricket and I came up to the state level, but my school never had a team because the founder, Jiddu Krishnamurti, believed that you should do your best, not because there is competition, but to do your best.'***

KFI was quietly seeding his future thoughts on education. Values like trust, affection for teachers, addressed as Akka and Anna (brother and sister), and the lack of using 'fear' as a tool for discipline helped foster his ideas of growth through freedom and empathy.

While many teachers inspired Damera during his school days, one memory stands vividly. He remembers his English teacher, Jayshree Akka, who once gave him 40 marks out of 100 simply because he forgot to write question numbers. When he approached her to argue for his case, she explained that if such oversights are ignored in internal assessments, he might repeat the same in the final ISC exams. Her intent was not to penalize but to instil a valuable lesson in attention to detail. He received an 'A' during the final grading. A life lesson learnt.

Many such experiences defined his outlook on learning. KFI helped lay a foundation for his belief system around education—a lifelong journey of growth and curiosity instead of a rigid framework which taught conformity.

FROM CHENNAI TO HARVARD—CHASING DREAMS ACROSS BORDERS AND BUILDING IDENTITY

While KFI broadened Damera's horizons, pushing him to rise beyond numbers and ranks, higher studies necessitated a switch to the CBSE-affiliated school, Vidya Mandir. However, this transition only deepened his reverence for KFI's unique approach to education. The next few years were not easy for Damera. Despite achieving a stellar 99.8 percentile, Damera was unable to secure an admission in any of Chennai's renowned colleges and instead enrolled in a B.Com. course at an evening college.

While this initially seemed like a setback compared to the traditionally celebrated career paths, life had other plans for him. This detour steered him in the direction of chartered accountancy, setting the stage for something far greater.

He soon switched from his evening classes to a correspondence course from Madras University, securing top ranks in CA intermediate and finals exams. He undertook internships and eventually landed a role in Citibank. After three to four years of excellence as a CA, Damera began to feel a strong urge to either start something of his own or make an impact on a much larger scale.

And it was Education that called out to him again. ***'One of my friends had gone to Cambridge, and I wondered why I never thought of applying abroad. Then my brother, who is also my role model, went to UT Austin to do a Ph.D. on full scholarship. He told me how great the education system was there, and I decided to experience it myself. I applied to four schools (Harvard, Columbia, Stanford and Wharton, and got into Harvard—my dream school.'***

If KFI played a pivotal role in shaping Damera's personal values and belief system, the two years at HBS completely transformed his professional outlook, nurturing an entrepreneurial mindset.

In the first few weeks, he could hardly believe that he was there. The imposter syndrome ran deep, and he often imagined someone from administration approaching him to say there had been a mistake and, that he had been admitted to Harvard due to some miscommunication and would need to leave. But as weeks passed, he gradually absorbed the reality and gained the needed confidence.

At Harvard, he had encounters with some of the brightest minds; individuals who had already started, expanded, and sold their businesses at great valuations even before entering HBS. This made him realise that he was among a cohort of extraordinary achievers.

Damera believes that incredible teachers throughout his life have played a big role in mentoring his academic rigor and acumen, and HBS was no exception. It was here that he met another remarkable educator—Kasturi Rangan. In one instance, Rangan gave Damera a grade of 2 (in HBS's grading system 1 is the highest and 4 is the lowest). Curious to know his grade was lower than expected, he asked the professor why he wasn't given a grade 1. The professor explained that while his answers were factual, they lacked the kind of depth and detailed assessment expected at Harvard.

Gradually, the knowledge-imparting techniques at HBS, deeply rooted in problem-solving through case studies, helped Damera to shift his focus. He became comfortable with not just looking for right answers but asking the right questions. He excelled in his work, narrowly missing the prestigious Baker Scholar's distinction by just a single A grade.

Damera also got inspired by another professor, Bill Sahlman, who taught him entrepreneurial finance. He considers Prof. Sahlman the 'Guru of Finance,' as his teaching style encouraged him to not chase the corporate ladder and venture into entrepreneurship instead. Another professor, Jim Sebenius, the founder of the Negotiation program, imparted invaluable lessons on how to negotiate effectively and turn the outcomes in his favour. In essence, the extensive and rich network at Harvard facilitated Damera's entrepreneurial instincts, urging him to take bold chances.

'A lot of the teaching at HBS was about doing and experiencing. A lot of people feel MBA is a waste of time,

as you just meet people and party a lot. I don't agree with this at all. I learnt a lot, partied, too, a little, but definitely learnt a lot,' he shared.

To everyone's surprise, Damera expressed a desire to join airlines—an industry which normally didn't recruit from Harvard due to its low salaries. Determined to break into the field, he wrote to the Dean of HBS (who was also a board member) requesting a summer internship at Jetblue. His persistence paid off, and he got selected, offered $10 for an hour for the role. During his internship, he shadowed his senior, the COO, and sat through multiple high-stake negotiations and gained valuable insights. This further sparked his ambition to become an entrepreneur.

Towards the end of his MBA, he got an offer from McKinsey but declined it. The fire of entrepreneurship burnt fiercely inside him, propelling his career in a new direction. It gave him the courage to step out of his comfort zone and pursue a path that was equal amounts exciting and uncertain.

Damera borrowed a framework from HBS, a teaching philosophy if you will, and applied it into his own entrepreneurial model while building Eruditus. This construct is encapsulated in the equation:

Career Success = Intellectual Capital (What you learn and how you learn) + Brand Capital (A good brand like HBS) + Social Capital (Who you know: your alumni, faculty, and peers)

This philosophy became the cornerstone of his business as he integrated it into Eruditus, a company which offers online education programs, aiming to offer career success to individuals seeking growth.

FIRST VENTURE—FAILURES, LEARNINGS, AND A STRONGER COMEBACK

'Maximum learning happens when your "self" and "situation" don't align. If they both line up, you are on autopilot, and we all gravitate to our comfort zone. So, put yourself in challenging situations early on in your career.'

At HBS, during a business plan competition, Damera brewed a revolutionary idea of creating a website for Indian hotels, flights, and holiday packages, meeting diverse needs of travellers under one roof. This idea got him the second position, further motivating him to turn his entrepreneurial dream into a flourishing reality.

While his parents, like any parent would, urged him to choose McKinsey's job offer, he decided to pursue his desire to venture into the world of start-ups with the intention to make things easier for people. The support from his HBS colleagues, Ankur Daga and Krishna Mahesh, who offered to invest $150,000 in his start-up further cemented his belief in this idea. Post his graduation, instead of staying in America to pay off his student debt faster, he took the risk and moved back to Mumbai. Wanting to turn his idea of a website for travellers into a reality, he founded Travelguru in 2005 with his HBS classmate, Ganesh Rengaswamy.

The idea of an online travel website quickly grabbed eyeballs in the Indian travel and tourism industry. The company raised $10 million from Battery Ventures and Sequoia Capital in two rounds of funding and became India's top online aggregator for hotels by 2007. In 2008, the raging popularity of Travelguru gained an offer from Expedia which wanted to acquire it.

However, things were about to change, not with one blow, but with two devastating ones. First came the global financial meltdown triggered by the subprime crisis and bankruptcy of global financial services firms hitting headlines and severely impacting several industries.

More tragically, November 2008's terror attacks left a fear of travel among the country's citizens leading to a decline in hotel reservations. As Travelguru's business model at the time revolved around hotels, it left a huge dent in its operations.

Due to the series of unfortunate events, their earlier negotiations with Expedia were called off. Travelguru was eventually sold to Travelocity at a fifth of the price Damera had initially negotiated with Expedia, resulting in a significant professional and financial setback.

Thinking back, Damera believes one of the key reasons for the failure of Travelguru was that while he was enamoured by entrepreneurship, he personally didn't share a deep love for travel.

Due to the terms of the sales agreement, he was required to stay with Travelocity for one year to ensure a smooth integration and transition, exactly the time he needed to reassess his interests and priorities. It was during this year that he realized that the education sector had always been his true calling.

THE BIRTH OF DAMERA'S TRUE DREAM—ERUDITUS

'I often say I measure my success by the number of people whose lives have been positively impacted by my existence. I knew I had to help people. In fact, at HBS, at the end of it, Josh Margolis, our leadership professor, asked us to write our life's principle in one line. Even today, mine is to give. The whole idea has always been to help.'

Considering the education system, Damera saw an opportunity to assist people to transform their lives. Searching for a deeper purpose, he crossed paths with Chaitanya Kalipatnapu, and both immediately connected on their shared belief of accessibility of education.

Chaitanya had earlier spent three years building simulations for INSEAD executive education, allowing him to get an understanding of the industry and helped him build an industry network. Inspired by their model, he went on to pursue INSEAD's MBA program, and upon graduating, came back to Mumbai to start something of his own.

Executive Education was a billion-dollar industry back then, with an increasing number of individuals eager to push their professional development to greater heights. However, as it necessitated attending classes from university campuses, many people, especially from developing regions, found it impractical to spend large sums in travelling abroad to attend these programs. To remove this gap, Damera and Chaitanya decided to gather the necessary resources and collaborate with the right people to bring campus-level education directly to people at affordable rates.

In 2010, five years after Travelguru, Damera and Chaitanya laid down the foundation for Eruditus Executive Education to empower Indian professionals to easily advance their careers. Then, came the point to decide how to enrol the participants and what exactly to offer.

'At that time, HBS was doing a four-day executive program and charging around Rs 1,60,000 in Hyderabad. We thought about who would pay for this in India and decided to do an eight-day program for Rs 40,000 rupees.'

While the idea was pushed into motion, both the leaders were surprised to see the lack of enrolments, despite the affordability of the program. HBS's program, which was priced more than double of what they were giving, had fifty to sixty participants, whereas they could only get twelve. This failure demanded a deeper analysis in order to launch themselves more successfully.

During the discussion, an HR executive voiced his opinion, saying that getting enrolments for an HBS program was much easier for him, as (a) it came with a brand value which individuals could leverage to propel their career, and (b) they offered certificates to validate the skills and knowledge of an individual. This made Damera and Chaitanya realise the value of branding and certification in the education industry.

Determined to move forward, they decided to partner with an established institution for their next offering. However, gaining the trust of the market rulers as two fresh faces was no easy task. After knocking hundreds of doors and facing rejections for six months, finally INSEAD, Chaitanya's alma mater, decided to give them an opportunity. In 2011, Eruditus launched its first co-branded executive MBA program with INSEAD, which they marketed as a year-long program with eight instruction modules and an aspirational peer group.

INSEAD had targeted thirty-five participants, but to their surprise, Eruditus was able to roll in fifty-five. INSEAD's belief in Eruditus and the Indian market grew. The program ensured three weeks of education at INSEAD campus and five weeks in India, with the same one-week-per-month for eight months calendar structure. At this point, for the smooth execution of in-person learning courses, Eruditus became the first education partner of TATA and CISCO's telepresence services. This form of communication allowed the participants to gather in a room and learn live from a renowned university faculty member, without facing the issue of latency.

Designed to help functional leaders become CXOs, the first module heavily emphasized the aspect of 'unlearning'. ***'Some of our participants actually cried in those few modules because it was too much. Very successful guys were told how badly their peers perceived them.'***

Initially uncomfortable to handle, the participants opened up gradually which made the learning process easier. The small success of this program set the stage for a company that now runs more than 70 per cent of its business globally.

Leveraging INSEAD's success, Damera was able to establish partnerships with Wharton Business School,

Columbia Business School, and MIT Sloan. By 2014, Eruditus staff had grown from two founders to a staff of thirty highly competent individuals, facilitating programs with limited seats from the top business schools globally.

However, Damera was also aware that once a business model hits markets, competitors emerge in numbers quickly. Something he had closely experienced with Travelguru. This was the reason why he now wanted to create a substantial and easy-to-scale and difficult-to-replicate model. But Eruditus was asking internal questions around more growth and stability, and that led to the birth of its sister company: Emeritus.

SCALING BUSINESS AND DREAMS—THE LAUNCH OF EMERITUS

Professor Vijay Govindarajan, who taught in Tuck School of Business, had developed a 'Three-Box' strategy framework which influenced Damera to incorporate it in his professional and personal lives.

Govindarajan's compelling framework offers drive for innovation without compromising daily goals. To put simply, box 1 means managing the present, box 2 implies selectively forgetting the past and box 3 focusses on challenging oneself and creating the future.

Damera saw this strategy perfectly mirrored in their situation. Box 1 meant continuing the existing executive programs with partners like INSEAD, Columbia, Wharton and MIT; Box 2 pushed them to unlearn their assumptions that premium education couldn't be democratized; Box 3 challenged them and set the stage for a global, tech-driven platform that could offer Ivy-calibre programs at a fraction of the cost.

In 2012, Coursera got into an agreement with Stanford University to launch several of their courses online exclusively. Several months after that, Harvard and MIT also joined hands to launch a platform, edX, to offer a wide range of their courses online. This made Damera think, 'Why can't we also offer online courses?'

Initially, Damera and Chaitanya approached Sloan School at MIT, Columbia School, and the Tuck School of Business at Dartmouth University to partner with them and launch a bunch of online courses. The idea was that intellectual content will be provided by the partner schools' faculty Emeritus would design and take care of the other aspects like filming, handling postproduction, marketing, arranging course leaders for live sessions, and facilitating student services for the enrolled.

All these schools agreed to contribute to the online offering and many experts expressed eagerness to join the company full-time, leading to the successful launch of Emeritus, a subsidiary of Eruditus, headquartered in Singapore in 2015.

A decade ago, most educationists were focussed on offering MOOCs (Massive Open Online Courses). However, Damera didn't want to blindly follow the trend. He aimed for much higher course completion rates and wanted to ensure that applicants applied their learning to real-life business problems. Hence, he decided to offer SPOCs (Small Private

Online Courses). They were inclined towards cohort-based programs that included live interaction rather than self-paced, isolated learning.

In addition, he ensured that all the programs incorporated project-based assignments to spark creativity and foster practical application of knowledge. Additionally, he introduced routine feedback practices from the faculty, so the participants weren't just graded superficially but guided and pushed in the right direction to enhance their capabilities.

That said, dominating the Indian education sector with Emeritus involved a lot of hit and trial decisions. They first introduced their leadership and strategy courses online, which did exceptionally well previously under Eruditus. However, this plan didn't work, and they had to end it.

On a closer look, Damera realised that individuals were not looking for basic building-block courses; they demanded something more focussed. Something that could enhance their skills and market value. As a result, they launched a course on design thinking next with MIT Professor Steven Eppinger, and a digital marketing course with David Rogers from Columbia Business School. These two quickly grabbed the eyeballs and became Emeritus' bestselling offerings.

With the exponential growth in India, and in the U.S. and regions of Latin America, the need to build a stronger global online presence emerged. By 2017, the team of Emeritus understood that they could successfully run in any part of the world as long as they could teach their courses in the local languages. This further escalated the brand's growth across the globe, making it one of the key drivers of the global edtech market since its launch in 2015.

'Every three years, we come up with an impact study, where out of 4000-5000 students who participate, 90 per cent would say that the program helped their careers, 85 per cent would say that their skillset improved, and 75 per cent would say that they will refer to their network. We have these metrics, and we publish them.'

In many ways, Emeritus emerged out to be better than a mere business expansion. It was the reality of how Damera and Chaitanya reimagined education would look like in the 21st century—borderless, affordable, and flexible.

THE VISION GOING FORWARD—THE DREAM IS STILL UNFOLDING

Today Emeritus stands tall as a global edtech leader, but the journey is far from over for Damera and his team. With technology changing at an unmatched speed and impacting industries in ways more than one, Emeritus intends to delve deeper into innovation, deliver personalized programs to meet diverse consumer needs of different age groups and stay ahead of the curve.

'From a business perspective, we are very B2C focussed, so we wanted to also support enterprise led growth because that's also a way in which you can impact lives. We want to do more in India, with Indian schools particularly. Since

we learnt a lot on design and delivery, we believe we can do a lot here with Indian schools.'

Damera also has his eyes set on the study-abroad business segment but not in its current form. He aims to disrupt it with his own innovative offering. For instance, one of the products they are developing would allow Indian students to do two years of coursework online in India through a US institution, earn credits for that and for the third year of the undergrad program, more than thirty abroad institutions would ideally accept their credits and welcome them in their university. This way, the cost of an undergraduate program from an international university becomes less than half.

Moreover, Damera at this point is in no hurry to plan an exit, sell his business, or file for an IPO. His focus remains firmly on democratizing high quality education for everyone. While he continues to innovate within the sector, he is thoughtfully considering what could the 'Box 3' be for himself and the future of Eruditus and Emeritus.

Education, for him, is not about shortcuts or quick exits. It's the deepest form of transformative change that individuals can see in themselves, often after years. That makes their mission even more urgent in today's times of tech led displacement of jobs and career related uncertainties.

CHAPTER 7

The Dawn That Shaped India's IT Education

Rajendra Pawar, Founder of NIIT

'He saw the future in code and built a nation ready to write it.'

TALES FROM THE PAST—THE MAKING OF A VISIONARY

Today, anyone aiming to build a rewarding career in IT looks at one name—NIIT, National Institute of Information Technology. From meticulously curated short-term certifications to comprehensive degree programs, NIIT continues to hold a premier position in the IT education and job landscape. But behind the tall and sturdy walls of this institution, however, lies the hard work, relentless effort, and exceptional vision of its founder, Rajendra Pawar, rightfully hailed as the father of IT Education in India.

Born in 1951 amid the lush landscapes of Jammu, Pawar grew up in a middle-class Dogra Rajput family with a deep tradition of service and courage. His father and all his father's brothers served in the Army, creating an environment shaped by discipline, duty, and a natural reverence for the land and its surroundings.

During his early years, Pawar loved spending time in fields, and whenever permitted, he accompanied his father to various places he was posted across Jammu and Kashmir. His eventual move to Gwalior also came because of one such posting, marking the beginning of a new phase in his formative years.

Amid this constantly shifting backdrop of his Army life, the memories of home and land became his quiet anchors.

Though Pawar's father built a home in Jammu, their ancestral roots lay in a small town called "Akhnoor", with the Chenab flowing just a few kilometres away. The land was not very fertile, yet the family kept the connection alive—more as an inheritance of identity than agricultural utility. As a child, he was introduced to the hobby of hunting flying birds, accompanying his father who would take him out into the fields during vacations. These early exposures to land, forest, greenery, and raw beauty of nature are memories Pawar holds close, shaping the nature lover and farmer in him—a deep rootedness to the soil that continues to define his everyday life.

Most importantly, the idea of leaving his homeland never appealed to Pawar. From turning down a UK scholarship in school to choosing not to apply to foreign universities for higher education, he always knew he wanted to bring a transformational change in his own country. Even today, he feels deeply connected to his ancestral land and often reads and reflects on the complex history of Jammu and Kashmir.

Along with sharing a profound bond with his land, Pawar has always displayed remarkable leadership qualities. Whether it was in school as a prefect, at IIT as the hockey team captain and president of students' council, or later in the industry as president of Manufacturers Association of IT for two years, and then chairing NASSCOM, these are the moments that stand as clear reminders of his ability to naturally lead.

The desire to help people without any political ambition runs in the entire family. His grandfather acted as a village leader who guided and supported people. His father, a softspoken and widely respected man who was spiritual rather than religious, became the head of 'Dharmat Society', the custodian of temples across the region. And his brother in-laws, who served the Army as commandos, paratroopers, and in military intelligence, also left a strong imprint on him, shaping his purpose and duty.

This close kinship to the land continues to bind the family together. Their family home built by their father stands as a symbol of these enduring values. While nobody lives there, it is constantly renovated and preserved so that its walls continue to hold the rich, shared memories of the Pawar family.

The Journey to Scindia School: Early Education and Lasting Impressions

The grounding Pawar absorbed from his family found further expression during his years at The Scindia School—

an institution that laid the foundation for his academic prowess.

There, he nurtured his intellectual curiosity, refined his leadership and analytical abilities, and engaged in several experiences that helped shape his remarkable personality. One such instance was addressing the school's persistent water scarcity. Driven by his gratitude for nature and connection to his land, he played a prominent role in reviving the taals (ponds) around the campus, an early example of his problem-solving abilities.

Another defining experience was an everyday ritual at the school known as 'Astachal', which means sunset hill. Each evening, the boys would dress in crisp white kurtas and pyjamas and gather in the amphitheatre during twilight to immerse themselves in the beauty of the sunset. Beyond offering a sense of calm, this ritual encouraged deep introspection, inspiring individuals to reflect on the day and their lives and plan the course of their future.

Although he cannot trace back his inclination to establish NIIT from his formative years, the combination of his school education and value-driven environment at home certainly steered him into eventually securing an admission at IIT Delhi (Indian Institute of technology, Delhi).

BREATHING THE AIR OF TECHNOLOGY—FROM IIT DELHI TO THE CORPORATE WORLD

Pawar's entry into one of the most prestigious engineering colleges in India is itself evidence of his academic excellence.

After completing his schooling from Scindia, Pawar enrolled in B.Tech. in Electrical Engineering at IIT Delhi. There, he not only gained theoretical knowledge but also immersed himself in the institution's culture, which emphasized systematic inquiry, teamwork, and solving real-work challenges.

It was here that he first experienced collaborating on projects, engaging in enlightening debates, and staying constantly aware of global trends. These years laid the foundation for an individual adept at developing innovative solutions, a mindset that played a pivotal role in his transition to the IT industry and the eventual founding of NIIT.

After graduating from IIT Delhi in 1972, Pawar made an entry into the corporate landscape as a Graduate Industry Trainee at Larsen & Turbo (L&T) in June of the same year; a role that grounded him in large scale project discipline and innovative thinking. However, after acquiring some of the essential core engineering skills, he made a seamless transition to the world of computing at DCM (Delhi Clothes & General Mills) as a Management Trainee.

In the early 1970s, DCM was known for identifying and nurturing strong managerial talent through its management training scheme. Often referred to as "Tatas of the North", DCM operated through several divisions, with textile division run by Dr Bharat Ram and chemicals and manufacturing overseen by Dr Charat Ram. The trainees were hired centrally, trained together, and then allocated to units best suitable to their abilities. In 1972, Pawar was placed in the textile division, marking an enlightening chapter in his professional journey.

DCM Data Products was another prominent division in the company, one that attracted exceptional talents such as Shiv Nadar and other renowned names. By around 1975, the group branched out to set up their own venture which first took shape as HCL Microcom and later evolved into Hindustan Computers Limited.

'When I joined HCL in 1976, I was involved in setting up the western regional office, and soon after in 1979, I moved to its corporate office. Since HCL was a startup at the time, it appeared as a fascinating place, and it is still one of the few renowned companies that operate with a startup mindset. While I didn't have a burning desire to become an entrepreneur, at some point, I decided I wanted to do something different, something of my own.'

Pawar left DCM in 1976, after four formative years to join HCL, initially to run a region and eventually to lead corporate planning. His time there allowed him to understand the intricacies of operations and develop a sharp sense of how to balance talent supply with the fast-shifting demand for talent.

Abiding by work requirements, Pawar also extensively travelled to several conferences where he realized the opportunity of the world computerizing was inevitable, especially for India. He could deduce that as the demand for computers grew in the country, so would the requirement for skilled individuals who knew how to program, drive and use computers. He could estimate how the gap of the skills could constrain the growth of the company.

'So I had the occasion to observe the seniors, Arjun Rutra and Shiv remotely as management trainees, but only in '76 when I joined HCL, '76 till '79, those three years I worked very closely with Shiv Nadar. And I hold even today that he's one of the smartest entrepreneurs the country has created—silent, quiet, but extremely brilliant and creative.'

During his time overseeing the corporate planning function, Pawar found a significant mentor in Shiv Nadar, whose guidance deeply influenced his early professional design thinking. Nadar would later become the Founding Chairman of NIIT, playing a pivotal role in shaping its conceptual foundation, an influence that continued to guide Pawar as the idea of NIIT began to take form.

That said, excellent mentorship combined with his own realization that the country's future success relied on creating a talent pool of tech experts as much as high end technologies, led to the founding of NIIT (National Institute of Information Technology) in 1981, an institution that championed the art of producing a consistent pipeline of IT-ready professionals.

NIIT: THE WHY'S AND HOW'S BEHIND THE FOUNDING OF INDIA'S LEADING TECH INSTITUTE

After his stint at HCL, Pawar realized one thing—challenges are opportunities in disguise. The constraints that the world faced, particularly in terms of lack of human capital in India's growing computer industry, became the genesis for the establishment of NIIT.

Initially, he decided to use a part of a consulting firm's office for a few months, before renting a space in Delhi. However, finding a suitable partner to turn his dreams into reality became more challenging than renting a place in Delhi. When Pawar was in Mumbai (then Bombay) in HCL, he caught up with his IIT batch mate, Vijay Thadani, who was then running Keltron operations for Western India. The two brilliant minds exchanged notes and engaged in insightful discussions about the role of technology in learning, unintentionally weaving the threads of an extraordinary partnership for the future.

He approached Thadani, urging him to leave his job and join his venture. By that time Pawar had observed a crucial challenge—there weren't enough professionals to work on computers, because there were no teachers to teach them in the first place. So, to solve this problem at scale, they were certain that they had to lean on technology.

Keeping all of this in mind, Pawar founded NIIT in 1981, with operations fully established a year later in 1982. By then, Vijay, who was in Bombay had already left his previous firm. And since they thought that Bombay was a developed market in many ways, most receptive of new ideas, they decided to start NIIT's operations there first. It became the testing place. Soon after, they got Rajendran on board, their junior from IIT, and that's how three visionaries came together to set the course of NIIT in the three-prime cities of Delhi, Bombay, and Chennai.

From a financial perspective, NIIT focused on a self-sustaining financial model from the very beginning. Instead of relying on venture capital for seed funding, founders leveraged their own savings, maintaining a clear focus on cashflow and profitability from day one. This approach ensured that the institution retained the creative freedom and culture of discipline, promoting organic growth. However, some small loans were taken from banks for expansion and sustenance.

Innovations in Products and Programs: Addressing the Emerging Needs

When NIIT was first launched in Bombay, in Nariman Point, in early 1982, it started with two BASIC courses. One was an entry-level, four-week long BASIC course aimed largely at students to introduce them to the basic concepts of programming. The other was a twelve-week, long-term course, designed to teach the COBOL language. While developing these courses, Pawar and his team were clear that they would go beyond the surface level programming, delving into the foundations of data, and most importantly, PLNT (Programming, Language and Technique), areas no one else was covering at the time, to create holistic-future-ready courses.

To impart knowledge, NIIT initially started using videotaped material from the U.S., created by a company called Advanced Systems Incorporated (ASI), known for lending their repository of learning materials to corporations and institutions. However, it soon became clear to Pawar that accent would be a concern for the Indian learners. Hence, they decided to build extensive support guides, called student guides and coordinator guides to simplify the courses, and make learning highly effective.

Pawar has always believed that they were in the learning business, not the teaching business, an important distinction. After all, in the teaching business, one focuses on the teacher whereas in the learning business, the focus is on the learner.

Words like 'faculty' and 'teacher' have never been used in NIIT history. From the beginning, it was always a "learner-centred, objective-driven" course. Their model included video instructions, a coordinator, and a learner, eliminating the need for a conventional teacher-student relationship hierarchy. Students were expected to first watch the videos, then solve problems listed in the student guide, respond to the questions posed by the coordinator, and then move to the computer room to put the learnings to practice. To further ensure that each individual received adequate attention, the batch size was deliberately limited to twenty-four individuals.

That said, the admission of the first few batches was the result of smart advertisements that NIIT had invested in. At the time, placements were scarce, and students, even from the IT sector, had to often wait for months after their college to land a decent job. Hence, Pawar knew the pain points of the unemployed generation; all that was required was to spread the word about NIIT in the most persuasive manner. That's exactly what they did!

'If you have a college degree and no job, this ad can change your life.' One simple, direct line that hit the learners exactly at the right spot, and that's how NIIT got its first batch of curious learners. What actually set NIIT as a leading technology institute in Bombay was the keen focus on learners and never-witnessed-before learning methodology. While initially there were enrolments from college students, soon the professionals from various companies started showing interest too, eager to enhance their skill set and become a part of the growing technology sector of India. Many MBAs, for instance, had the best of marketing knowledge but could sense the employment segment undergoing a technological shift, motivating them to gain expertise in computers and information systems.

With computers gaining momentum in professional spaces and hinting at an evolution of workforce, CEOs too started approaching NIIT to widen their spectrum of knowledge and offer the needed training support to their employees. Consequently, along with enrolling college individuals and working professionals, within the two years of its launch, NIIT had done a program for the chairman and executive directors of Indian Oil.

After two years, Pawar realized that instead of approaching those seeking jobs, they should go on campuses and capture the attention of curious students wanting more knowledge. This small thought eventually became a game-changer as it led to the creation of the dual-qualification program.

Following this idea, to attract the best minds to NIIT, Pawar and his team began conducting quizzes, enticing winners with free courses. They succeeded since there existed a growing need for computers on campuses. Soon, almost every higher learning institution from across different locations started contacting NIIT resulting in the need for the institute's expansion to other states.

Emergence of Franchisees? No, Joining Hands With Business Partners

The idea with expanding and building franchisees is that one man cannot be in so many places. Besides, Pawar realized that building layers of management between the central team and individuals running the centre could dilute the entrepreneurial spirit at the point of contact. This is probably why they decided to never use the term 'franchise' and instead focused on developing business partners, establishing a carefully curated 'win-win business-partner model'.

As a result, Pawar and his team decided to set up centres across cities in partnership with like-minded people. However, to ensure that each centre delivered the same high-quality standards consistently, they designed a structured operational process and maintained control over the layout and interiors, ensuring all centres shared a uniform look and feel.

Next came the challenge of selecting individuals who would be willing to take ownership, which meant finding the right students and smoothly running the programs, without compromising the quality. By that time, NIIT was also doing six-month programs and in response to the growing needs, they expanded to one-year, highly extensive programs. To ensure they chose the right candidate, someone willing to invest their time, money, and energy, they conducted surveys, trained people, and ultimately, selected the most eligible from a pool of twenty to thirty candidates in each city.

These individuals were mostly from small towns, hailing from reputed, wealthy families, who had moved to cities to do something of their own and make it big. The selected candidates went on to gain recognition for their contributions in digital literacy and job creation.

PHASES OF DIVERSIFICATION: FROM CONSULTANCY AND EDUCATION TO SOCIAL INNOVATION, UNIVERSITY EXCELLENCE, AND AI-ENABLED GLOBAL SERVICES

After successfully establishing nine centres across India through its business-partner model, NIIT launched its first software distribution system, under the brand Insoft. It was also during this period that Arvind Thakur, an alumnus of IIT Kharagpur, 1975 batch, joined NIIT as the fourth co-founder. He brought the expertise to set up a structured methodology for seamless execution of NIIT's consulting services, and it was under his guidance, that the consulting arm reached greater heights, garnering immense respect for delivering consistent, measurable outcomes.

Over the next few years, famously labelled as the 'hospital-college' model by several experts due to its visionary founders, NIIT's consultancy and the software arm acted as the 'hospital' and the training segment became the 'college', preparing students for in-demand industry skills. The real innovation was NIIT's ability to extract industry insights directly from college projects and continuously adapt the curriculum, ensuring the courses remained highly relevant in the constantly evolving job market.

By the early 1990s, NIIT was ready to take its learning model to foreign lands. In 1991, it set up its first office in the United States, with IBM as one of its earliest clients. From there, the company smoothly expanded across Asia through its learning centres, whereas the US and Europe became strong markets for its corporate training and software business services. While establishing a strong international presence, NIIT continued to diversify and strengthen its learning models in India as well.

In 1992, the institution took the major step by formalizing its educational offerings with the launch of GNIIT (Graduate NIIT), a comprehensive program aimed at producing industry-ready IT professionals. This transitional shift from short-term courses to long-term, industry-aligned courses firmly positioned NIIT as a leader in skill development.

The following year, in 1993, the company was listed on the stock exchange, unlocking the resources that strengthened its expansion and solidified its position as a pioneer in the IT education industry. During the 1990s and early 2000s, NIIT also engaged in several mergers and acquisitions, including the acquisition of Element K and Osprey Systems, strengthening its corporate training and e-learning capabilities. However, many of these acquisitions were later concluded to keep its focus strictly on imparting knowledge and skills.

NIIT Foundation: Expanding Access, Enabling Futures

In 2004, NIIT Group launched its social development arm called NIIT Foundation, created with the purpose of taking quality education and skills beyond conventional, privileged classrooms to underserved learners.

Today, the organisation reaches 2 million learners each year, including 1 lakh youth trained in employability programs, achieving an impressive 70 per cent placement rate. Its nationwide presence spans over 600 outlets learning outlets—NF centres, partner centres, Digital Buses, and HIWEL stations—ensuring deep last mile across urban, semi-urban, and rural India

NF offers a wide spectrum of programs covering digital literacy, foundational skills, AI, cybersecurity, data skills, IT/ITES, retail, BFSI, life skills, and entrepreneurship, enabling holistic capability-building for diverse learner groups. Trusted by many corporates, NGOs, government bodies, and community organisations, it has earned a reputation for delivering a high-quality, scalable impact across the country.

Blending inclusive pedagogy, scalable digital models, and strong governance, NF drives measurable impact across schools, colleges, and communities. Its initiatives develop future-ready capabilities in emerging technologies while ensuring access for women, PWDs, LGBTQ+ communities, gig workers, and rural youth. Above all, NIIT Foundation remains committed to advancing equitable opportunity and sustainable development across India.

NIIT University: Shaping Thinkers, Innovators, and Leaders of Tomorrow

Almost two decades after the launch of GNIIT, Pawar and other founders decided to strengthen their commitment to higher education by allowing NIIT to branch into NIIT University in 2009. In contrast to GNIIT which doesn't offer formal degrees, NIIT University was launched under UGC as a full-fledged degree-granting university, offering a wide range of diploma, degree, and doctoral courses in the space of technology and management. By blending academic rigor, research, innovation, and its long-standing industry connections, Pawar was able to execute his vision of building a workforce equipped with in-demand, industry-relevant IT skills, leaving no room for industry-academia gap.

NIIT University, often referred to as the "University of Future", is one of the greenest campuses in Rajasthan. Since its inception, the university has upheld a remarkable track record of ensuring placements for every student before convocation—a commitment that remained unwavering even during the tumultuous period of covid.

As they strengthened NIIT's legacy to make its identity truly distinctive, ensuring that the institution remained "technology-based, industry-linked, research-driven, and seamless". The institution has also been deliberate in selecting its visionary leaders. Dr Karan Singh was the first chancellor who retained his position for ten years, followed by Dr Kasturirangan, with Amitabh Kant currently serving as the chancellor.

As NIIT continued to broaden its vision, it also partnered with National Skill Development Corporation (NSDC), launching initiatives NIIT Yuva Jyoti to empower youth and equip them with employable technology skills. Apart from this, the company diversified its business line, with ventures such as NIIT IFBI for the field of banking and training and NIIT Imperia for digital marketing programs.

Its Corporate Learning Business also grew steadily, especially through NIIT's Managed Training Services (NIIT MTS), which over a period has become a global offering for large enterprises seeking end-to-end workforce development.

NIIT MTS has built one of the most advanced AI-powered learning ecosystems in the industry by using generative AI to create and update training content at high speed, deliver personalized learning paths, enable virtual coaching, and provide real-time feedback to learners. The company was recently recognised as a market leader by the Fosway Group, Europe's leading HR industry analyst.

In 2023, NIIT strategically carried out its demerger. It transferred its Corporate Learning Business, including NIIT MTS to NIIT Learning Systems and retained its Skills and Career business under NIIT Limited. This allowed each entity to manage and consistently execute numerous visions and missions of Pawar and other founders, while maintaining a continuous pipeline of IT professionals.

A LEGACY OF NURTURING TALENTS THAT CONTINUES TODAY

It is often said that seeds of one's life work are sown in childhood, and for Pawar, those seeds were curiosity, resilience, and quiet determination shaped by the world around him. Carrying these values forward, he stepped into IIT Delhi with clarity of purpose that only deepened during his formative stints at L&T, DCM, and HCL. Overtime, his vision took clearer form and drew like-minded people who shared his belief in the transformative power of technology. United by a common purpose, they set out to make every individual technologically skilled and literate at a time when computers were only beginning to take root in India. The culture of upskilling, which today fuels a wave of edtech startups, was first introduced by Pawar through NIIT's pioneering short-term technology courses.

The foundation grew into something much larger; something no one had imagined. Through the establishment of NIIT, he democratized IT education in India and fostered a startup mindset through the business-partner model, while building an ecosystem where skill development, structured consulting, higher education, and software services seamlessly operated in parallel.

At the heart of this ecosystem, were the continuous innovations in products and services. While GNIIT program's strong corporate tie-ups helped create a workforce ready to fuel the country's software revolution, NIIT University laid the foundation for full-fledged, research-driven higher learning across numerous domains. NIIT's Managed Training Services (MTS) further expanded his vision by becoming a global benchmark for end-to-end workforce development enabling companies globally to upskill and reskill at scale. Parallel to this, NIIT Foundation has been carrying this mission to underserved communities, ensuring quality learning reaches those who need it the most. There was a time, when aspiring engineers or anyone aiming for a career in technology dreamt of NIIT as a gateway to success—an institution far ahead of its time.

Looking back today, his undeniable impact holds true to his title of father of IT education in India. His legacy stands as a testament to how one man's dream cannot only transform industries but also the destiny of generations. In every skilled-professional, every thriving company, and every higher-learning institution aspired by his vision, his vision continues to breathe and take new forms.

CHAPTER 8

The Trust That Shaped India's Coaching Industry

Dr J.C. Chaudhry, Founder of Aakash Institute

'One man's vision built an institution thousands could trust.'

A REVOLUTIONARY DREAM, A RELENTLESS VISIONARY

Across the nation, the name *Aakash Institute* shines as a beacon of ambition, discipline, and academic excellence. Yet behind the monumental success of this iconic institution lies the extraordinary journey of one man—Dr J.C. Chaudhry, the founder whose relentless vision and passion for teaching redefined India's coaching landscape.

Born in 1949 in Sevli, a small village in Haryana, J.C. Chaudhry's childhood was shaped by scarcity but illuminated by discipline. Education was revered in his family, though resources were meagre. Nights were often spent reading under streetlamps or by the flicker of a candle. Those formative years carved resilience into his character and planted the seed of what would one day become one of India's most influential educational empires.

In 1966, he left his village of Hathin to pursue Pre-Medical at S.D. College, Palwal. The transition was harsh. Coming from a Hindi-medium background, he suddenly found himself struggling in an English-medium environment. The first six months were filled with doubt, hesitation, and a constant feeling of being left behind. Yet he persevered.

Though he dreamt of becoming a doctor, his scores in the pre-medical exam weren't enough. In 1968, he pivoted, enrolling at DAV College, Jalandhar, for a B.Sc. (Medical). Later, he pursued an M.Sc. in Botany at Birla Institute of Technology and Science, Pilani. The journey was gruelling. He often travelled with just Rs 5-Rs 10 in his pocket, fully dependent on scholarships. It was during these years that his philosophy crystallized: mastery of fundamentals before tackling complexity—an insight he absorbed from a mentor, Mr S.S. Widge. This philosophy would later define the DNA of Aakash.

His early professional years were spent as a schoolteacher, and though modest, the classroom became his stage. His energy was infectious. Students adored his clarity. But more than that, they sensed his *nasha*, a passion for teaching so deep it felt like a calling.

That calling grew restless. In 1988, he made a leap that would alter the course of Indian education. With just Rs

2000, twelve students, and a rented room in Delhi, *Aakash Institute* was born.

SCALING TRUST, NOT JUST BUSINESS

If there is one principle that defined Aakash's rise, it was trust—not aggressive expansion, not immediate profits, but a slow, deliberate building of credibility.

Dr Chaudhry himself put it best:

'This wasn't a business for me because I knew a person only needs two pieces of flatbread to sustain their hunger. There was no greed for more. I only wanted respect, so I only worried about that. I was addicted to the high of teaching and to earn that respect back. That obsession turned it into what it is today.'

The 1990s were a time when coaching institutes mushroomed across India. Many poured money into advertising to draw students. But Aakash refused. Instead, it grew organically through results. The first batches cracked top medical entrance exams, and word spread like wildfire. Parents whispered recommendations at social gatherings, neighbours shared stories, and soon, the twelve student classroom multiplied. By the late '90s, Aakash was dominating Delhi's coaching scene.

The strategy was simple but powerful: deliver results, and trust will follow.

By the early 2000s, however, India's coaching landscape was changing. The IIT-JEE and medical entrance prep markets were exploding. Rival players like FIITJEE and Allen were making national moves. Around this time, a strategist advised him:

'Don't be dependent on one single city. The entire country should have your centres.'

This became the spark for national expansion. Between 2004-2006, Aakash went pan-India. Unlike the quiet growth of the 1990s, this phase was backed by large-scale advertising. When students secured top All-India Ranks, their faces appeared in eight-page newspaper spreads. The storytelling was sharp, students from small towns making it big, aspirants rising against odds, all guided by Aakash.

It was a masterclass in marketing.

FIERCE COMPETITION AND EDTECH DISRUPTIONS

As the 2000s advanced, the battlefield of Indian test prep turned ferocious. Legacy institutes competed with each other, while a new breed of edtech startups—BYJU'S, Vedantu, Unacademy—offered flexible, app-based learning at scale. Coaching, once limited to cities, was suddenly accessible everywhere.

Yet Aakash didn't falter. It thrived, fuelled by decades of earned trust. Unlike many others, it wasn't just selling a product; it was selling certainty, discipline, and a culture of rigor.

Even as Aakash expanded to 200+ centres across India, Dr Chaudhry insisted on personal visits. Faculty recalls him arriving in classrooms, listening to their feedback, motivating teachers, and even speaking with parents. This personal touch in a scaling business became a differentiator.

When entering the South, where schools were reluctant to allow coaching partnerships, his advice to his team was simple: write personal letters to principals. One line of 'I have come all the way from Delhi to meet you' opened doors.

Then there was his secret edge—numerology.

Often, when meeting school leaders or parents, he would offer personal guidance using numerology. What might have seemed mystical turned into a bridge of trust. People felt seen, understood, and supported. This blend of discipline and empathy was rare and often, unforgettable.

BEYOND THE EDUCATOR—THE NUMEROLOGIST

Few know that behind Aakash's formidable academic reputation, its founder had a parallel identity—as a world-renowned numerologist.

His fascination began in 1984, during a dinner in Haridwar with his brother-in-law. What started as casual chatter became a twelve-hour marathon on numbers, patterns, and destiny. Soon, he was experimenting.

A chance train encounter cemented his belief. Seeing 'Dharampal' tattooed on a co-passenger's arm, he did a quick calculation and narrated details of the man's life. To everyone's shock, it was spot-on. The entire coach buzzed with astonishment.

At home, experiments followed. His son, originally named Manish, was renamed Aakash after Chaudhry found the earlier name didn't align numerologically. The results, he insists, were undeniable.

By the time Aakash Institute employed nearly 7,000 staff, he conducted a numerological audit, discovering that 92 per cent were aligned with the organization's energy.

What began as personal practice soon became a mission. He wrote books *Advanced Numerology* and, *Practical Numerology*, launched the digital app known as JC Nummero, founded the Indian Institute of Numerology, and even created International Numerology Day. In 2022, he earned a Guinness World Record for hosting the largest numerology session.

For him, numerology was never superstition. It was an alignment. A way to channel energy, unlock potential, and bring clarity to choices.

THE BYJU'S ACQUISITION AND THE SPLIT

Then came 2021, a year that shook Indian education. COVID-19 had shuttered classrooms nationwide. Many coaching centres collapsed. But Aakash didn't. Years of early investment in digital ensured a seamless shift online.

Sensing an opportunity, BYJU'S approached. They assumed Aakash was struggling. But to their surprise, the opposite was true, Aakash was growing.

The outcome: one of the most iconic acquisitions in Indian edtech history. BYJU'S acquired Aakash for nearly a billion dollars in a cash-and-stock deal.

The industry was stunned. A thirty-year-old brick-and-mortar coaching brand had merged with a digital unicorn. On paper, it looked perfect: Aakash offered credibility and rigor, BYJU'S offered reach and technology. Together, they promised a hybrid model for the future.

But reality was less harmonious.

Cultural clashes soon emerged. BYJU'S was fast, experimental, and aggressive. Aakash was disciplined, structured, and methodical. Governance misalignments widened the gap. By 2024, the Chaudhry family withdrew from the merger application.

Later Aakash was sold in parts to Ranjan Pai's Manipal Group.

Meanwhile, Aakash doubled down on its own future. **Aakash 2.0** was born, a Rs 100 crore bet on digital, blending the institute's legacy rigor with cutting-edge online tools.

Lesson? Even billion-dollar deals collapse if values don't align.

BEYOND EDUCATION

In 2004, partnering with his eldest son, Dr Aashish, Chaudhry entered healthcare.

Aakash Healthcare was founded in Delhi, with a mission to offer affordable, patient-centric care. What began modestly became a leading super-specialty hospital in Dwarka, known for cutting-edge technology, compassionate doctors, and over a million patients served.

The values were the same: integrity, service, excellence. As he often said, 'Seva Parmo Dharma.'

Even beyond education and healthcare, Chaudhry's vision expanded into spirituality. In Vrindavan, he commissioned four magnificent temples—Maa Vaishno Devi Dham, Shiv Dham, Shani Dham, and Radha Krishna Dham.

In 2025, he earned another Guinness World Record for a 187-foot-long Trishul, an engineering and spiritual marvel.

For him, these were more than monuments. They were sanctuaries, spaces to elevate consciousness, preserve culture, and inspire devotion.

From a boy studying under streetlamps to the founder of one of India's most influential institutions, Dr J.C. Chaudhry's journey is nothing short of extraordinary.

He has worn many hats of being an educator, entrepreneur, numerologist, healthcare evangelist, spiritual architect. But through them all, one thread remains: service.

After all, something we can learn from his life's trajectory, purpose doesn't retire. Passion doesn't fade. Visionaries never stop.

SECTION 3

Changing Systems

In the age of ten-minute delivery models, education transformation is akin to a lifelong delivery model. Changing underlying systems and the accompanying ecosystem take vision, time, effort and collaboration at multiple levels.

In this section, read about the visionaries who approached Education from a systems lens. Reimagining institutions, skills and policies that would drive systemic change in Education for not just years, but decades ahead.

CHAPTER 9

From Wealth to Philanthropy—Offering Opportunities to All

Ashish Dhawan, Founder of ChrysCapital, Central Square Foundation, Ashoka University, and The Convergence Foundation

'He turned privilege into purpose, and opportunity bloomed for all.'

CHAPTER 1: PLANTING SEEDS OF PURPOSE—EARLY LIFE INFLUENCES

In the bustling streets of India's knowledge capital, renowned for nurturing some of the country's most intellectual minds, a young boy was laying the foundation for a path that would eventually make him one of India's highly intellectual philanthropists. Born in Delhi and raised in the warm, vibrant and intellectually stimulating environments of Kolkata, Ashish Dhawan understood the importance of academic success from an early age. During his years at St. Xavier's School, Kolkata, he was immersed in a culture of academic rigor and curiosity.

'I didn't do as well academically. I was a reasonable student till 8th grade, then I became a much better student 9th grade onwards. Because I understood the importance of doing well academically in order to get on to a certain trajectory'

His interests extended beyond the classrooms. He was equally invested in extracurricular activities. He was appointed house captain and spent hours each day playing badminton. Teachers nurtured his potential, allowing him to unravel his own capabilities in a well-rounded, enriching learning environment.

For instance, in 10th grade, during his first Math class test, Dhawan got 44 out of 65, while most of his classmates failed. Though the result initially left him disappointed, the experience proved transformative. The class was taught by one of Xavier's legendary teachers, Thomas Vienna, known for setting exceptionally high standards. His emphasis on precision, rigor and practice, instilled a deep appreciation for academic discipline in his students.

For Dhawan, this moment became a pivotal lesson in pushing his boundaries. Similarly, another influential figure in Dhawan's journey was Father Vishesh, associated with Xavier's for more than four decades. He had the ability to spot potential in students and motivate them to achieve what they thought was nearly impossible.

Beyond classroom learning, students were encouraged to read newspapers daily, helping them stay informed about Indian and global affairs. This habit, along with participating in impromptu debates, allowed Dhawan to sharpen his communication skills and significantly boosted his confidence.

One event that significantly influenced Dhawan's growth was organizing the annual school fest—Chrysalis. This event, which also welcomed students from St. Xavier's College, turned into a grand celebration, offering him plenty of hands-on-experience in planning, leadership and execution.

His emotional connection with the school festival formed a long connection with the event's name 'Chrysalis.' The term, which refers to the pupal stage of a butterfly, symbolizing protection and transformation before emergence, stayed with him. Little did he know during his teenhood that years later, it would inspire the name of his private equity firm ChrysCapital, formerly known as Chrysalis Capital.

Fittingly, the metaphor of a chrysalis echoes his own personal evolution. The values, disciplines, and life skills he acquired during his school years became the foundation for a transformative journey, one that would ultimately redefine the education landscape of India.

FROM KOLKATA TO IVY LEAGUES—BROADENING HORIZONS WITH GLOBAL LEARNING MODELS

At the age of eighteen, Dhawan expressed his urge to study abroad and left the city of Kolkata to explore international borders. His hard work paid off, and he got into Yale University (an Ivy League institution in the United States), where he majored in Applied Mathematics and Economics; the two disciplines that eventually became the backbone of his financial career.

'Yale was very different from schools in India. For me, it was freedom; not just in terms of being away from parents who couldn't monitor every movement of yours, but more importantly, freedom in terms of exploration of options. You could explore anything. You could do anything. There were no barriers. You could take a class in music theory, technology, astrophysics ... everything was available. So, it felt like a curious kid lurking in a mechanic store, you could sample as much as you want.'

But studying at Yale was more than just living an independent life; he was exposed to liberal arts and global perspectives. He could easily distinguish between the rote learning model quite evident in Indian education institutions and the freedom of expression offered abroad. Dhawan initially thought he would pursue engineering at Yale, but the multidisciplinary learning allowed him to understand his true interests.

For instance, during his freshman year, economist John Geankoplis, who was a professor there, introduced him to the world of economics, and Dhawan fell in love with it. Similarly, the other classes that he pursued in history and geo-political science sparked curiosity in him. In essence, this sampling of subjects gave him the opportunity to move beyond conventional learning models and career aspirations, and to discover his true calling by exploring multiple disciplines.

On his return from Yale, after interacting with his friends from India, he realized that they had had a completely different higher education structure. He had become a different person after his graduation; someone who now had the vision of bringing the global perspective of education to Indian classrooms.

Dhawan graduated from Yale in 1992 and began his career as an investment banker at Wasserstein Perella, a prestigious M&A advisory firm in New York. This experience helped him understand the processes of deal-making, mergers and acquisitions, and how businesses planned their growth. A year later, he transitioned into private equity at McCown De Leeuw & Co., a firm based in California, where he operated as the junior-most associate. There, he gained insights not only into how businesses were bought and sold, but also about value creation and how businesses were built, preparing him for his own investment and philanthropic journeys.

After working in the investment banking and private equity sector for three years, Dhawan returned to academia for his MBA, at Harvard Business School (HBS), undoubtedly one of the most prestigious business programs globally. In his experience, the environment of a business school was much more academically relaxed and practical, as it offered a lot of time to establish a strong network and become a global citizen.

'You learn to socialize with people from across the world. You learn to become more of an extrovert, how to small talk and engage with people,' he recalls while drawing a comparison between his formative years at Yale and his enlightening journey to Harvard.

In addition, when Dhawan was at Harvard, he gost a lot of time to reflect and think about the purpose of his life. There, he first decided to become an entrepreneur. Though he worked in a corporate setting for two to three years, Harvard ignited that little spark of business ownership when he was doing his master's. Post business school, he knew he wanted to pursue his first love—investing, but he was unsure which niche he would venture into.

At the same time, he also had the urge to have a second career, one that could help create an impact on society. He was clear that a career outside of the business world would be equally satisfying. Eventually, things unravelled in an organic flow, giving him a smooth path to follow.

THE BIRTH OF INDIA'S LEADING PRIVATE EQUITY FIRM—CHRYSCAPITAL

After graduating as a Baker Scholar—an honour awarded to the top 5 per cent of the class—from Harvard Business School in 1997, Dhawan joined Goldman Sachs, the American multinational investment bank and financial services company. There, he worked in the private equity division, which managed the company's own capital for private-equity style investments. The exposure and experience he gained there strengthened his confidence and served as a launchpad for co-founding his own private equity venture, ChrysCapital.

When Dhawan co-founded ChrysCapital with his friend Raj Kondur in India, the concept of building a world-class private equity firm was still quite unfamiliar in the country. India had liberalized its economy just a decade earlier, and the idea of private equity, though already highly successful in the U.S., was still alien and radical for many budding entrepreneurs. However, Dhawan saw an opportunity there: to offer capital, strategic thinking, and long partnerships to emerging businesses, and in doing so, take the Indian economy to unmatched heights.

What began as a modest business venture with a small team quickly grew into a firm with an unparalleled reputation. Why? ChrysCapital had a well-structured investment plan, which involved investing in companies operating in technology, healthcare, financial services, and business outsourcing segments. More importantly, what truly positioned them as a dominant force in India's investment market was its active engagement with management teams, commitment to long-term value creation, and strict emphasis on due diligence.

In the firm's early days, raising capital from foreign investors was a considerable challenge because: (a) private equity was a nascent concept in the Indian market, and (b) only a few global players were placing bets on Indian businesses. However, this is where Dhawan tapped into the networking skills honed at Harvard. He had already established his credibility as a Baker Scholar and had an extensive network in finance; He used them to do what many thought was impossible: convincing top U.S. endowments, including Harvard University and Stanford University, to back ChrysCapital.

Dhawan believes that his HBS professor, Jay O. Light, had a huge role in his destiny. Professor Light, as the chairman of Harvard Endowment, took a punt of 25 million dollars on Dhawan's venture and it worked out reasonably well. Stanford also played a major role. The experts in the U.S.A. wanted to get to know the Indian market and believed they could, through this fund.

Under Dhawan's meticulous leadership, ChrysCapital gained recognition for its sharp judgement and ability to identify high-potential ventures. By backing businesses like Infosys, Mahindra Finance, Bajaj Finance, HCL Technologies, and Shriram Transport, the firm not only gained hefty returns but also built a reputation for backing transformative businesses.

Beyond returns and valuations, Dhawan gained valuable insights from his journey at ChrysCapital—lessons he continues to apply in his current ventures. While strategic thinking and practical learning were imperative, the most profound lesson he learned was humility. As he puts it, being an investor means recognizing that it's ultimately the entrepreneur who creates the magic. The role of an investor is to work quietly in the background offering guidance, support, and fresh perspective while allowing the entrepreneur's vision to lead the way.

But for Dhawan, ChrysCapital was more than a financial success story; it was a masterclass in leadership, purpose-driven ambition and strategic thinking. By 2011, having achieved what most investors only imagine, he made an exit at the peak of his career, ready to embrace a new chapter: to help build the nation with the transformative power of education.

REWRITING THE RULES OF HIGHER EDUCATION IN INDIA: CO-FOUNDING ASHOKA UNIVERSITY

After leaving an irreplaceable mark in the Indian finance and business sector, Dhawan decided to dedicate himself to transforming education in India. While graduating from Harvard, he had sensed that his second act would be away from the business world. And here he was, all set to foray into the Indian education landscape, but with a solid purpose and vision.

His inclination towards education was shaped not only by his own academic journey abroad but also by a powerful influence from childhood—his grandfather, who had established more than fifty schools in Lahore and Delhi for underprivileged families. That legacy stayed with Dhawan and continued to inspire him over the years, ultimately encouraging him to start his own venture in education.

Around 2008, Sajeev Bikhchandani, founder of Naukri.com, approached Dhawan and expressed the idea of introducing an Ivy-League calibre institution in India. In no time, his dream of venturing into institution and nation building came alive; he decided to not only partner with him but actually take charge of the entire process along with him, Dr Pramath Raj Sinha, and a few others. For the next five years, he combined his wide global network, strategic thinking, operational discipline, and extensive experience to bring an interdisciplinary education model to India.

What happened as a result is a landmark in Indian educational history: the founding of Ashoka University. Built through extraordinary collective effort, the institution brought together more than 100 founding donors, each contributing not just funds but also their time, energy, and ideas. What makes Ashoka truly unique is its model of collective philanthropy: no single donor has more than a 1 per cent stake, ensuring smooth shared ownership and collaboration. To bring his vision to life, Dhawan constantly worked with a team of experts to ensure that India's educational needs aligned with global academic standards.

Dhawan believes that every job in today's world requires you to be interdisciplinary. This belief was a driving force in designing Ashoka University, where a student could choose both computer science and philosophy. He believes that if a student is only trained in one subject, they fall short on social consciousness and diverse perspectives.

Launched in 2014 in Sonepat, Haryana, Ashoka University, quickly became renowned for its interdisciplinary approach, global faculty, and academic rigor. It attracted thousands of the brightest minds from across the country and introduced them to a transformative model of education; one that emphasized critical thinking, research-based learning, and socially engaging teaching techniques. The approach stood in sharp contrast to the conventional rote learning still prevalent in traditional colleges.

For Dhawan and other founders, it was more than just founding a university—it was achieving something deemed impossible earlier: combining visionary leadership and philanthropy to reform the higher education landscape of India. The goal was always to introduce Indian students to the idea of gaining autonomy over subject selection by encouraging them to try their hands at multiple disciplines before making well-informed choices. The whole concept of choosing a subject based on personal interest and experience, rather than predetermined paths, was new to Indian students who had relied on the guidance and beliefs of their elders when making career choices earlier. Through this shift, they realized the power that comes with taking control over one's career journey.

The founders of Ashoka wanted it to become a role model for other universities and that's exactly what happened when the National Educational Policy (NEP) of 2020 demanded every institution to follow an interdisciplinary teaching model.

CENTRAL SQUARE FOUNDATION: DHAWAN'S CONTINUING JOURNEY IN EDUCATIONAL PHILANTHROPY

'The man who dies rich dies disgraced', a quote from Andrew Carnegie's book *Gospel of Wealth*, inspired Dhawan into recognizing his privilege and ability to do more. Even before

Ashoka University was officially launched, Dhawan had begun his philanthropic journey by founding Central Square Foundation (CSF) in 2012. After working for years in the private equity sector, he turned his attention to addressing the gaps in the Indian education system, and that meant starting from the foundation level.

CSF came into existence as a non-profit foundation with the aim of ensuring that each and every child receives quality school education, irrespective of their background. Dhawan understood that without mastering basic reading, writing, and arithmetic, most kids would inevitably struggle to progress in the higher grades, leading to poor academic performance and consequently, higher dropout rates. This scenario was particularly evident in low-income families, where parents worked hard to send their children to school, only to see them drop out later due to low performance. Hence, he wanted to make sure that such students built a strong educational foundation, helping them stay engaged in learning and ultimately secure employment, breaking the vicious cycle of poverty.

However, rather than running schools directly, Dhawan chose to partner with state governments, education departments, educators, and fellow non-profit organizations to bring a massive change at the system and policy level. His mission was clear: intervening and offering support in terms of edtech integration in classrooms, teacher-training, curriculum and assessment reformation, and evidence-based policy changes.

What truly distinguishes CSF from other non-profit foundations is that it applies a venture capital mindset to the segment of philanthropy, similar to a VC funding and supporting startups. However, in case of philanthropic projects, the results are measured in learning outcomes and social impact created, not financial returns. For instance, CSF supports high-potential non-profit ideas and facilitates their adoption on a state-level by offering continuous strategic guidance, multi-year funding, and well-curated roadmaps.

Dhawan's efforts to make Foundational Literacy and Numeracy (FLN) a priority in NEP 2020, resulted in the government announcing the National Initiative for Proficiency in Reading and Understanding (NIPUN) Bharat Mission. As per this initiative, it has become important for every child in the country to attain FLN skills by Grade 3.

When he exited ChrysCapital in 2011, many people assumed that he had retired, because not many considered philanthropy as a career choice. Even today, the misconception persists for many. However, Ashish's journey is a testament of philanthropy as a career choice and not merely a path someone pursues when they retire at an old age.

THE CONVERGENCE FOUNDATION (TCF)—LEVERAGING CSF LEGACY FOR A NATION-WIDE IMPACT

'We believe that India has a missing middle. Hundreds and thousands of NGOs are on the ground doing good work but it's their own work. It's not scalable but very good in terms of discovering the problems and coming up with solutions. However, they often can't get it embedded, and governments can't scale it. 'Think Tanks' are very

good with ideas, but they are not good at pushing the idea and converting it into a policy. So, there is this space in the middle which is downstream from the think tanks and upstream from NGOs. I realized this through CSF and decided why not create thirty CSFs across different sectors.'

After almost a decade of building and empowering the nation through his widely acclaimed ventures like Ashoka University and Central Square Foundation, Dhawan realized the humongous impact he could achieve by introducing multiple variants of CSFs across various sectors of the country. This notion led to the birth of The Convergence Foundation (TCF) in the year 2021. As a philanthropic platform, it goes beyond addressing challenges in the education landscape. Its aim is to transform the lives of all Indians through rapid and sustained economic growth and inclusive development.

TCF supports mission-driven institutions that are focused on long-term social and developmental concerns, aiming to deliver systemic impact. It essentially covers three domains: accelerating economic growth, enhancing human capital, and advancing development enablers. The first domain focuses on accelerating economic growth by fostering an attractive investment climate, boosting exports of goods and services, developing cities and regions as growth engines, strengthening tourism, and advancing science and technology.

The second domain focuses on enhancing human capital, with an emphasis on improving education, skilling, apprenticeships, labour mobility especially overseas employment, and women's economic empowerment.

The third domain, as Dhawan calls it, advancing development enablers, focuses on strengthening institutions of state capacity, building organisations that can catalyse population-scale improvements, and enhancing strategic philanthropy. Today, the TCF network consists of over twenty mission-driven organisations that work at the system level to move the needle on complex issues and create impact at scale.

In essence, TCF bridges the gap between civil society, private sector, and the government. Dhawan, through this foundation, aims to achieve his vision of institutional nation-building—one that aims to empower the nation not through charity, but by motivating entrepreneurs to engage in the social sector and contribute to India's holistic growth, while accelerating their own personal as well as professional growth.

'I'm a believer that economic development trumps everything else. So, firstly, every child in India should have basic education. As children transition out of school, at least half of them should undergo apprenticeship and internships to learn by action. This is the best way to develop your skills and attitudes. Theoretical skilling, on its own, I believe, is useless.'

Ashish Dhawan firmly believes that India's growth can be driven by leveraging philanthropic contributions, especially in the space of education. Everything is interconnected. For India's economic development to take priority, it is essential to build a human capital base that is equipped with 21st century skills, acquired through interdisciplinary education.

CHAPTER 10

Getting to the Core, Changing Systems

Anita Karwal, IAS Officer and Secretary, Department of School Education, Ministry of Education

'From policy into possibility, a beacon of progress.'

FROM ROTE TO REAL LEARNING—A TRANSFORMATIONAL JOURNEY FROM SCHOOL TO COLLEGE

Though she never envisioned herself as academically exceptional during her formative years, destiny charted a different course. Little could she have imagined that she would eventually retire as the Secretary of the Department of School Education, Ministry of Education, a position from which she would fundamentally reshape India's K-12 education landscape.

Anita's upbringing was shaped by parents who regarded education as a transformative force, a conviction they were determined to instil in their children. Her father, a distinguished civil servant in the Indian Revenue Service, held a master's degree. Her mother, although she had set aside aspirations for higher education to pursue homemaking, harboured an insatiable thirst for knowledge. Eventually, she pursued her graduation alongside Anita's elder sister, remarkably outperforming her own daughter.

'My father was resolute that we two girls (my brother was born eight years after me), should receive the finest education possible. My sister, two years my senior, enrolled directly in grade 1, as kindergarten did not exist then. I joined the same class along with her at age four. My parents adjusted my birth year, enabling me to be with my sister and to complete school by sixteen. My father's transferable position did not always guarantee access to premier institutions, but he moved mountains to provide us with every opportunity.'

What might surprise many is that young Anita was a reserved yet profoundly creative individual. Throughout much of her schooling, in her own words, she excelled as a 'rote learner' with exceptional memory, though ironically, she retains little of that memorized content today. While grappling with concepts like the refraction of white light through a prism, which she does not quite understand till today, her parents recognized her creative inclinations and encouraged exploration beyond conventional academics. This nurturing environment allowed her to embrace her artistic nature, delving into writing and painting with abandon.

At eight or nine years old, she submitted a poem to the *Hindustan Times* that was published, a validation that ignited a passion. She began contributing regularly to *Children's World* magazine, allowing her creativity to flourish unfettered.

Her parents championed these creative pursuits and her fascination with nature, shielding her from societal prejudices. Growing up in the 1970s, when female education remained uncommon, Anita considers herself fortunate to have had progressive parents who recognized and nurtured her talents. She vividly remembers achieving the gold medal for the top rank in Zoology Honours at Delhi University, and the profound pride radiating from her father. Yet despite her achievement, newspapers overlooked her accomplishment while celebrating male toppers from her university, a stark reminder of the unequal recognition women received for academic excellence.

Nevertheless, college marked Anita's intellectual awakening, a transition from rote memorization to genuine conceptual understanding. Previously reliant on her prodigious memory and recall abilities, she discovered the confidence to engage deeply with her studies. Her professors introduced hands-on learning and experimental methods. For the first time, she genuinely savoured academics and, in the process, discovered authentic learning.

The collaborative learning environment proved equally transformative. Anita frequently taught juniors and peers, which not only reinforced her own understanding but also enhanced long-term retention, a pedagogical principle she would later champion professionally.

However, the initial transition from her secure home environment was not seamless at all. Before Daulat Ram, she had enrolled at a different Delhi University college and hostel, where she experienced profound culture shock.

'There was this binary in those days; colleges were branded either "behenji colleges" or "smart colleges," and I definitely fit the "behenji" category because I was overly simple in my physical appearance and reserved. I also discovered substance abuse at that particular college. My father was then serving as India's Narcotics Commissioner, so I understood the chemistry of every substance from his discussions. That is when I told him that I could not continue there, which led to my shift to Daulat Ram College for girls, where I felt genuinely comfortable.'

At Daulat Ram, the welcoming atmosphere eased the challenges of separation from family in Gwalior. From someone intensely protective of her privacy, she blossomed into a woman who formed meaningful bonds with peers and faculty. College life undeniably transformed her into a more self-aware, collaborative individual. From academics to social connections to her love of physical well-being, every dimension of Anita's personal evolution took shape during those formative years.

She particularly cherishes memories of two close friends from the History department and the enduring friendships they forged. She also fondly recalls a lecturer who tragically passed away from illness during her third year, a teacher who encouraged them to embrace curiosity and witness the true magic of science.

After completing her bachelor's in Zoology with the University's top rank, her curiosity drew her to political science, prompting a master's degree, where she ranked third at Delhi University. Simultaneously, she pursued a three-year diploma in French. Her appetite for expanding her intellectual horizons and exploring diverse disciplines remained insatiable. She subsequently pursued an MPhil in African Studies.

'All I knew was an insatiable appetite for learning. I was not following a calculated path. I was following my curiosity. Political science because my friends sparked my interest. African studies because an inspiring professor opened that window. I was driven by pure joy in discovering new disciplines and expanding my intellectual horizons. Sometimes the most meaningful journeys are those we do not plan meticulously but rather allow ourselves to fully experience.'

While others perceived her path as meandering, Anita was learning and loving the journey. She was collecting ideas, crossing disciplinary boundaries, deliberately stepping away from conventional linear trajectories to lay the foundation of a mind capable of navigating complex policies, ultimately positioning herself to redefine India's educational future.

AN UNPLANNED DREAM—THE CASUAL, UNSCRIPTED ENTRY INTO CIVIL SERVICES

'My friends took it upon themselves to procure the application form for me. I remember one sitting beside me, literally dictating what to write where. I was not even confident they would deposit the filled form, but I received an admit card, and that is how the entire journey began.'

At twenty-one, while pursuing her MPhil, Anita noticed classmates preparing for civil services examinations. When they questioned why she wasn't following suit, especially given her father's distinguished career, she experienced a moment of profound reflection. She realized her father had never imposed his aspirations or directions upon his children; he had always wanted them to discover their own authentic callings. Nevertheless, yielding to peer pressure and curiosity, she asked friends to obtain a form for her, and almost whimsically, she entered the world of civil services.

She cleared the examination in 1986 on her maiden attempt, securing an allocation to the Indian Revenue Service (IRS). During training in Mussoorie, she met her future husband, Atul Karwal. She felt content with the opportunities the IRS offered. For someone who considered herself laid-back and unambitious, securing a position in such a prestigious service, especially with her father as her superior, felt like an extraordinary blessing. However, Atul encouraged her to attempt again and aim for the IAS, which would enable her to serve people more directly.

Though initially resistant, because joining the Indian Administrative Service often meant relocating to remote areas, far away from family, her husband's conviction persuaded her. She appeared for the examination again in 1988, cleared it, and joined the IAS. Even after succeeding, she hesitated to join but eventually received her first posting in Bihar, followed by Gujarat.

Bihar, her home state, presented formidable challenges. Posted as an officer trainee at Palamu in the then-undivided Bihar, she discovered a deeply conservative environment, one where women in authority were not readily accepted. Drawing stark contrasts between Bihar and Gujarat's governance, she observed that while Gujarat was much more forward-looking and operated with remarkable efficiency, Bihar was still grappling with huge administrative issues. When she was transferred to Gujarat after a year, though she admired the strength and clarity of its governance, mastering the local language became her next hurdle. By the time Karwal became a Sub-Divisional Magistrate (SDM), she had acquired linguistic fluency and confidence.

More importantly, she had begun cultivating a leadership philosophy that would define her entire career. She takes immense pride in having empowered her subordinates, not merely as a management technique, but as a core value. She believed that true leadership was not measured by the authority one wielded, but by the confidence and capability one instilled in others. Whether it was a junior clerk in a district office or a senior colleague navigating complex policy decisions, Karwal made it a point to create an environment where every individual felt valued, heard, and equipped to excel.

She understood that organizational success was fundamentally a human endeavour, and that sustainable change could only emerge when people at every level felt ownership and agency in their work. If there is one legacy she hopes to leave, it is precisely that: being remembered not for the policies she drafted or the positions she held, but for the dignity, respect, and opportunity she extended to everyone she encountered, a testament to her belief that how we treat people ultimately matters far more than what we accomplish.

She takes immense pride in having empowered her subordinates. If there's one legacy she hopes to leave, it's precisely that: being remembered for how she treated everyone she encountered.

A GRADUAL FORAY INTO THE EDUCATION LANDSCAPE

After serving as an SDM in Gujarat, Karwal ascended to District Development Officer (DDO) of Zilla Panchayat in 1993, assuming responsibility for primary education districtwide. She spent an entire year immersing herself in the system, understanding its nuances from the ground up. One conviction crystallized during this period: the necessity of strengthening teacher education and providing proper infrastructure to students and faculty—essential foundations for creating lasting impact through educational reforms.

After nearly four years as DDO, she was appointed State Programme Director of an NGO called Mahila Samakhya, dedicated to empowering girls and women through education. Working across five districts, she was assisted by district heads in each location. They worked directly with women and girls in every school, providing training and maintaining continuous engagement.

This program allowed Karwal to comprehend the intricate details of the entire educational process. It began with understanding why mothers themselves neither pursued education nor sent their daughters to school. As she built relationships, she discovered that women lacked family support, making their daily routine of multitasking overwhelming. To address this, the NGO encouraged entire families to learn together, an approach that proved remarkably effective. The crucial role of the family in the education of a child was deeply ingrained in her.

These two experiences marked Karwal's entry into India's education sector. From there, she served in several pivotal positions: Collector, Deputy Municipal Commissioner of Ahmedabad, Secretary (Education) at the state level, and later in Delhi as Joint Secretary in the Ministry of Education, Chairperson of the Central Board of Secondary Education (CBSE), and ultimately Secretary of the Department of School Education, Ministry of Education.

Throughout her thirty-six years in the Civil Service, she has been most passionate about her sixteen-year journey, where she got the opportunity to work in the school education sector and contribute to the reforming of India's education landscape.

Karwal has maintained that education must be approached with a socio-emotional lens—one requiring heart and soul at every step. She emphasizes that every child, teacher, and school is unique, and success lies in finding common threads to unite these diverse elements. That said, she acknowledges that her own understanding evolved gradually. Initially, as DDO, she would push teachers to introduce academic rigour, homework for repetitive practice and regular tests to help students improve in specific subjects. However, as her understanding deepened, she transitioned from this results-driven approach to embracing the principle that all learning begins with socio-emotional stability, and unless it is joyful, relevant, and contextualized, genuine engagement with learning becomes improbable.

She came to understand that educational reform begins with teacher training, their empowerment and motivation, and ensuring that all leadership from the top to the bottom supports teachers' efforts. She recognized the importance of engaging families and investigating deeper barriers to children's education. Inclusion became central to her philosophy. She firmly believes that until every child has access to high-quality education, equality and equity remain mere rhetoric. Every factor affecting a child's growth and development, whether it be the medium of instruction, nutrition, physical and mental health, access to educational resources, school safety, personal hygiene, or public sanitation, demands equal attention to create the enabling ecosystem every child requires to participate meaningfully in their education. This realization struck Karwal during her NGO work, prompting her own evolution into a more emotionally attuned, socially conscious reformer.

Transition from State to Central: From Gujarat to Delhi

'I discovered that education remains undervalued in bureaucratic cultures across states, treated as a lesser assignment rather than the transformative opportunity it truly represents. Few approach it with the passion and excitement it deserves, which is precisely why those who do can make an extraordinary impact. I also observed the vast diversity in how states operate, their unique routines, procedures, and levels of efficiency. Gujarat's meticulous attention to detail set a benchmark I aspired to help replicate nationwide. The challenge was not in pointing out gaps, but in building trust and demonstrating possibilities. Gradually, through collaboration rather than criticism, states and Union Territories began embracing a shared vision of educational excellence.'

For nearly two decades, Karwal's professional learning was deeply rooted in Gujarat's governance landscape. After decades of district and state-level service characterized by a no-nonsense approach and decisive leadership, she received her Delhi appointment, which would become the most defining phase of her professional journey. This represented more than geographical relocation. It was a fundamental shift in responsibility. From optimizing policy execution at the state level, she would now shape policies for nationwide impact.

Her initial steps in Delhi involved bridging administrative gaps to establish necessary uniformity in policymaking and execution nationwide. She began engaging states and Union Territories more collaboratively. She understood that ensuring minimum standards across the country required a foundational framework. Additionally, process simplification was essential. The culture of reform and transformation became paramount, and she credits her success entirely to her highly efficient teams she can count on even today.

Gradually, her persistence yielded results. She began receiving positive responses from all states and Union Territories, facilitating alignment with the broader vision of educational reformation. This groundwork prepared her for the chairpersonship of CBSE in 2017, a role that positioned her as a key driver in transforming India's education landscape and impacting the lives of millions of students.

THE TURNING POINT—BECOMING CHAIRPERSON OF CBSE

'Education is the most dynamic field imaginable. If a day passes without challenges, you are simply not engaging deeply enough. Every layer you peel back reveals new dimensions requiring attention, new problems waiting to be solved. That is not a burden; that is the privilege of working in a sector that shapes millions of lives. The complexity is precisely what makes it so vital, so alive, and so endlessly rewarding.'

Merely one month into her CBSE chairpersonship, while still grasping her responsibilities, news of two paper leaks dominated headlines, with media sensationalizing the incident and demanding her immediate removal. Instead of capitulating, Karwal embraced the challenge positively, deciding to thoroughly examine every aspect of the conduct of examinations.

From understanding how question papers were prepared, what the criteria for evaluation were, where answer sheets were printed, how questions were selected, to secrecy protocols, transportation logistics, and storage locations, Karwal left no stone unturned in creating comprehensive Standard Operating Procedures (SOPs). An able Controller of Examinations in CBSE was able to match her pace of reforms, idea by idea, implementation by implementation. These same SOPs remain in force today, ensuring paper leaks are no longer a concern.

When Karwal assumed office in CBSE, a committee formed at the Ministry level was already drafting the National Education Policy (NEP), with early versions emerging. She began identifying areas for meaningful reform. As NEP discussions progressed, she realized that genuinely reforming school education required fundamentally rethinking assessments. Changing teachers' mindsets and encouraging pedagogical shifts necessitated overhauling the curriculum structure from its foundations.

To initiate this process, Karwal and her team introduced the first wave of assessment reforms in 2018, incorporating competency-based questions in exam papers with a planned

10 per cent annual increase. Consequently, 60 per cent of current CBSE exam papers have done away with rote-based assessment and focus on knowledge application and real-life scenarios.

Other significant reforms introduced by her in the Board include, introduction of innovative pedagogies such as experiential learning, mandatory sports sessions every morning across all grades, special exams for school children participating on behalf of India in international sports, project-based learning through SEVA, school quality assessment framework, creating school clusters as Hubs of Learning, structured teacher capacity building programs, integration of technology in almost every aspect of functioning of CBSE, etc.

In 2019, CBSE became the world's first education board to mandate Artificial Intelligence as a skill subject from grade 8 onwards. This move catalyzed a series of progressive reforms that have become cornerstones of India's evolving education landscape.

Today, regarding curriculum development aligned with NEP and the National Curriculum Framework (NCF), numerous reforms are being adopted across CBSE. Curricula for grades 1 and 2 are already implemented, grades 3, 4, and 5 are substantially in place, and the grade 6 onwards curriculum is currently in progress.

As Secretary in the Ministry of Education, Karwal continued her push for and focus on assessment reforms beyond CBSE. Significant reforms were implemented at the National Institute of Open Schooling (NIOS). The processes

Karwal and her team introduced at CBSE were mirrored at NIOS to ensure no procedural gaps hindered open learning efficiency. Since formal education is mandatory until fourteen in India, NIOS begins at class 9. NIOS began adopting the NEP-curated curriculum. Moreover, NIOS is aligned with formal education in skill development, focusing strictly on vocational education. Consequently, NIOS students are finding employment and building rewarding careers more readily.

For other state boards, and other boards like ICSE and IB, Karwal initiated the establishment of the NEP-based PARAKH, or the National Assessment Centre, now housed within NCERT. It guides other boards toward high standards of curriculum transaction, including assessments, such as the one unleashed in CBSE and beyond. Additionally, this centre helps standardize educational procedures, assessments, and security systems nationwide, ensuring greater consistency and quality in school education.

For instance, CBSE under Karwal's tenure began offering two assessment attempts per subject, allowing students' better scores to improve overall results. These innovations are gradually being adopted by state boards under the aegis of PARAKH. Significant credit belongs to Karwal and her team, whose vision and groundwork set these changes in motion.

TAKING OWNERSHIP OF NEP DEVELOPMENT

The National Education Policy (NEP) 2020, one of India's most discussed reforms, arrived thirty-four years after the first education reform in 1986, marking a historic milestone. It signalled the Indian education system's readiness to embrace change and evolve. When Karwal served at CBSE, NEP discussions were gaining momentum. However, concerns about ownership and direction existed within the ministry. The then-Secretary asked if Karwal would assume ownership and help develop the NEP, to which she gladly agreed.

The NEP development work demanded time much beyond office hours. Karwal and her team would often work on it till late into the night, sometimes even up to midnight, discussing and planning each word, each sentence, each chapter in the policy.

During this period, Karwal was introduced to Dr Kasturirangan, who chaired the NEP drafting committee. He was already known for his brilliance in the space research field, but what made Karwal his fan follower was his deep understanding of the educational requirements for India for the present and the future. He ably guided the NEP drafting committee to give India its most path-breaking education policy of all time.

When the first draft emerged under his guidance, it was posted online to invite suggestions and feedback. Karwal was entrusted with analyzing every comment, which required close collaboration with team members, including the NCERT director and NIOS Chairman. Together, they sifted through more than 150,000 responses, identifying exceptional ideas, many of which were incorporated into the final document.

Subsequently, Karwal was appointed Secretary of the Department of School Education, though NEP remained unreleased. After a thorough feedback review, discussions with the Prime Minister commenced.

'The depth of scrutiny and the countless hours the Honourable Prime Minister dedicated to examining every dimension of the policy were extraordinary. His uniquely transformative vision for school education draws from extensive grassroots engagement across India and his distinguished stewardship of education in Gujarat. His unwavering commitment to girl child education, equal educational opportunities, oral fluency, and his pioneering introduction of thematic universities in Gujarat—innovations that remain unparalleled elsewhere in the country—informed numerous critical aspects of the policy. He demonstrated a rare ability to bridge aspirational, forward-looking frameworks with ground-level realities. Many of his recommendations were remarkable in their implementability and their authentic connection to grassroots needs. These insights proved so valuable and contextually relevant that they were woven into the fabric of the final policy, enriching its practical applicability while enhancing its visionary scope.'

Karwal vividly recalls sitting outside the cabinet room on 29 July with the then Secretary looking after higher education. As electronics were prohibited inside, both carried documents, prepared to present evidence if discussions arose regarding any aspect of NEP approval. While mentally preparing their arguments, news suddenly emerged from the cabinet: the policy was approved. According to Karwal, the wave of relief and excitement was indescribable, a triumph after years of effort and unwavering dedication.

Following approval, they were instructed to hold a press conference explaining policy details in both Hindi and English. Though Karwal commanded excellent English and Gujarati, she spent two hours before the conference preparing her Hindi remarks, ensuring clear, confident delivery. To their pleasant surprise, not one person during the conference or in subsequent newspaper coverage questioned the policy. Remarkably, even opposition parties praised NEP's smooth development, acknowledging its potential to positively shape future generations.

While the policy was released in 2020, Karwal emphasizes that extensive research underlying its formulation has made it so comprehensive and forward-looking that it remains relevant today and will continue for years to come.

For NEP implementation, a detailed plan called SARTHAQ (Students' and Teachers' Holistic Advancement Through Quality Education) was created to guide NCERT, state/UT governments, CBSE, Kendriya and Novodaya Vidyalayas, state boards, and every school and education governing body on implementation strategies. The NCF was introduced in two parts: the first in 2022 when Karwal served as Secretary, and the second in 2023 just after her retirement. While SARTHAQ provided the implementation roadmap for NEP, NCF specifically addresses the policy's fourth chapter, covering curriculum, pedagogy, assessments, and related areas. Given the extensive reliance of states on SARTHAQ as their implementation guide, Karwal emphasizes the importance of keeping it dynamic and continuously updated to reflect evolving ground realities and emerging best practices.

Beyond SARTHAQ, she highlights the Nipun Bharat policy addressing literacy and numeracy skills, which has been extraordinarily well-received nationwide. Its implementation is also systematic and sustainable. She feels that the fact that NIPUN Bharat has a very flexible, yet innovative implementation framework may have contributed to its nationwide success. In her view, sustaining NEP's long-term impact requires constantly developing locally relevant and contextualised frameworks and constantly updating them in accordance with the demands of the times. Regular revisions, she believes, help ensure states effectively align with the broader vision.

Similarly, NISHTHA (National Initiative for School Heads and Teachers for their Holistic Advancement), a program started by Karwal's predecessor, was designed to support teacher training and professional development. During COVID, under Karwal's initiative, the program successfully transitioned to online learning. Since its implementation, it has received tremendous response, with nearly 100 per cent of teachers in almost all states completing it. In total, Karwal and her team structured approximately 140 initiatives following NEP's launch, detailed in the booklet "*Two Years of NEP.*"

Possible Challenges Ahead in NEP Implementation

Karwal estimates another five years before the policy's true impact fully manifests. However, potential challenges might impede continuous implementation across different states. Alongside leadership deficiencies, she believes the primary challenge is mindset, not of teachers but of educational administrators. Teachers are eager and capable of transformation, but policy administrators must alter their conventional thinking.

Second, since NEP emphasizes holistic education, including student skilling, multidisciplinary approaches, experiential and project-based learning, teachers require excellent quality training to deliver these goals. Third, foundational literacy and numeracy must be prioritized, as the success of subsequent stages depends on getting this foundation right.

Fourth, she highlights the often-overlooked preparatory stage (ages nine to fourteen). She believes this critical period for adolescents, when they naturally begin exploring, questioning, and rebelling, receives insufficient attention. According to her, this phase fundamentally shapes a child's trajectory, determining whether they become job creators, job seekers, or risk becoming dropouts.

Finally, Karwal firmly believes nothing succeeds without assessment reforms. In our current system, she observes, teachers teach to test, whereas the genuine focus should be skill and knowledge acquisition. Only if core concerns are addressed with urgency and sincerity can NEP's true potential be realized for this generation and those to come.

WHAT LIES AHEAD FOR THE PASSIONATE EDUCATION REFORMER

'I have learned to trust and surrender before life's unfolding journey. Rather than rigidly mapping every step ahead, I embrace the present with openness and curiosity, two things that have guided me throughout my career. My husband and I believe in staying grounded in the now, allowing opportunities to reveal themselves organically. It is a philosophy of purposeful presence rather than anxious planning. It is about being in the now and enjoying it.'

Post-retirement, Karwal has assumed a five-year tenure role in government with multiple responsibilities. She currently serves as Chairperson of Gujarat's Real Estate Regulatory Authority (RERA). She is also the Chairperson of the Standing Committee of Pandit Deendayal Energy University. Additionally, she is Vice Chair and Managing Trustee of the Gujarat Energy Research Management Institute (GERMI) and heads Gujarat's Advisory Committee on NEP Implementation for Higher, Technical, and School Education.

While Karwal continues embracing life's opportunities, she initially planned to launch her own school education initiative, offering insights and analysis to those seeking guidance. However, it was not to be, or so she thought before assuming her current roles. But somehow, numerous schools and educationists began contacting her for support, keeping her completely occupied. That is when she and a friend, who herself is a renowned educator, decided to start their own podcast, entitled NEP-Tunes. It is the only podcast of its kind which explains the conceptual and implementation aspects of the NEP and the NCF in-depth. Alongside, Karwal continues to help all those who call on her for help and support, because she believes that for education to have an all-around impact, innumerable hands will be required, both government and non-government.

Her connection to this field runs so deep that she envisions dedicating herself to it for the rest of her life, continuing to contribute meaningfully long after formal appointments conclude. Beyond education, she nurtures her creative spirit through writing. She has authored and co-authored several acclaimed works spanning both fiction and non-fiction. Most recently, alongside two co-authors, she has been chronicling insights on education itself. Their sequel to "*The Power of Curiosity*" has just been submitted for publication, a testament to her belief that learning and sharing knowledge are lifelong pursuits.

Parallel to her professional accomplishments runs an equally profound spiritual journey that began when she was just eight years old. This inner path continues to awaken and empower her, providing the peace and clarity that have anchored her through decades of public service. Her spiritual inclination was deeply nurtured by her mother, a woman of quiet strength and wisdom, whom she lost to cancer when her mother was only fifty-eight. That loss deepened her understanding that life's true wealth lies not in positions held, but in the peace, we cultivate within and the impact we create around us.

When asked what advice she would offer aspiring civil servants and education reformers, Karwal's response carries the weight of hard-earned wisdom:

'Education is not just a fascinating sector. It is the most consequential one. This is your moment to enter it, to fuel it with strategic vision and heartfelt support, to enable every child to discover and reach their unique, holistic potential. Those who choose this path today will touch the lives of millions of students in ways both profound and beautiful. And I can tell you from experience: there is no greater joy, no deeper fulfilment, than empowering those around you to become the best versions of themselves. That is legacy. That is purpose. That is a life truly well-lived.'

CHAPTER 11

Blueprints of Change

Pramath Raj Sinha, Founder of Ashoka University and Harappa

'He didn't wait for change … he became the change he wished to see.'

HOW HUMBLE BEGINNINGS HELPED FORGE A VISIONARY MIND

Before embarking on his journey of enlightenment, Sinha was just a boy growing up in Patna, Bihar, surrounded by ink-stained pages, the whirring sound of printing press machines, and the deeply rooted norms of a traditional Indian family.

India's humble towns have nurtured many of the nation's great visionaries. The story of Dr Pramath Raj Sinha, a reformer who transformed the landscape of higher education in India, is no different.

Hailing from a lineage of famous Hindi writers and poets, his father Udaya Raj Singh, had established a printing press to publish the celebrated literary works of his grandfather, which eventually evolved into a successful family venture. A few years into the venture, he launched '*Nayi Dhara*', a publication that emerged as a disruptor in the 1950s. Known for publishing some of the most influential writers at the time, including Harivansh Rai Bachan, Ramdhari Singh Dinkar, Mahadevi Verma, Amrita Pritam, the magazine also became a vital source of income for many writers. Seventy-five years after its launch, *Nayi Dhara* is undergoing a digital transformation under Pramath's meticulous guidance, expanding into audio and video formats and reimagining its social media to resonate with an audience shaped by contemporary consumption habits. True to its name, which translates to new currents, *Nayi Dhara* continues to evolve while staying rooted in its original spirit.

The fourth child and only son after three much older sisters, Sinha was raised in a closely-knit family where his father entrusted him with several responsibilities from a very young age, instilling in him a mindset of "getting stuff done", whether through hard work or negotiation.

Despite the wide age gap, Sinha's sisters have been the guiding lights and role models for him for as long as he can remember. Challenging societal expectations, Sinha's eldest sister, Manjari Jaruhar, broke barriers by becoming the first woman IPS (Indian Police Service) officer from Bihar, at a time when women were barely allowed to pursue an education. Her journey, marked by determination and relentless hardwork, left a deep impression on Sinha's mind.

Observing her excellence and watching her transform her father's mindset, Sinha learned to form his own opinions, away from the more traditional trappings of the society.

THE IIT YEARS: FROM CURIOSITY TO FAILURES AND SUBSEQUENT CLARITY

After completing his schooling at St. Michael's High School, Patna, Sinha followed what was then considered the most ideal career path by enrolling in IIT Kanpur. However, his rank, which earned him a spot at the institute, made it difficult for him to study the subject he wanted to. This experience made him realise the education's landscape's obsession with ranks, and how it jeopardized students' futures.

'It is ridiculous I think that in today's day and age, that you are good enough to get into an institution, but you are not good enough to study what you want to.'

Influenced by his brother-in-law's footsteps, Sinha initially decided to pursue aeronautical engineering. However, when he got into the counselling session, the counsellor suggested he considered metallurgical engineering instead, implying that he had a rank good enough to secure a place in a more "practical" department.

At IIT, Sinha observed something truly baffling: individuals would retake exams to improve their switch from one department to another, such as from mechanical engineering to electrical engineering, all because of the limited number of seats. This practice deeply impacted him, and it became a guiding principle for him at Ashoka University, where he made sure that students would never have to endure such rigidities.

That said, his first few semesters in engineering were quite challenging. While he was fighting a severe case of Jaundice and as a result struggling to focus, the faculty seemed more concerned with his grades than his well-being. The combination of declining health and pressure to perform took a toll on his scores, leaving his report card filled with Cs and Ds. This marked his first career setback and made it clear to him that he wasn't going to top his department.

Nonetheless, Sinha believes not many people realise that IITs are great examples of liberal education. At the core of their foundation is the idea to expose students to all disciplines of engineering and electives in humanities and social science before they specialize and this aligns with the fundamental philosophy behind liberal arts education.

One such course 'Introduction to Computer Programming' fuelled Sinha's curiosity, and he excelled in it. Later his final year project involved a lot of programming, giving him the opportunity to connect with the right professors, helping him strengthen his grasp of complex theories which he had failed to grasp in his classes. While he was making progress and his grades had improved significantly, he still couldn't envision himself working as an engineer in the long run.

FROM PATNA TO PENN

Even after tasting success in computer programming, Sinha remained convinced that engineering wasn't for him. He attempted the CAT Exam but did not get a top score for an IIM. Still, he wasn't disappointed as his real goal was to go to the US to pursue higher studies. Though he got a decent GMAT score, he couldn't get into the top schools.

Thanks to the programming course and successful project he had completed, he fought for a chance to be considered in Tata's campus recruitment drive. Despite being from metallurgical engineering, he was able to demonstrate and drive attention towards his programming skills, which impressed the recruiters and eventually helped him receive a job offer from them. But as he was getting ready to start his job, two of his professors intervened. They advised him to continue his education and pursue a master's degree at least instead of getting into the corporate sector.

One of the professors, who had earned a Ph.D. degree in mechanical engineering from Penn, offered to recommend his name. Sinha had always harboured the dream of going to Wharton. Motivated by the opportunity and guidance by the professors, he decided to apply to Penn for a master's in mechanical engineering and was accepted.

But then came the financial struggle: he couldn't get a scholarship for his program. Despite limited finances, his father encouraged him to go by selling some of his land and borrowing some money from his daughter, who was already well-settled in the U.S. The Sinha family came together, pooling their resources and support, to push him closer to his dreams.

To ease the burden of his family for semester fees and other living expenses, he began working multiple jobs. He worked four roles:

1. As part of Penn's film society, he worked odd hours projecting films in society run theatres while simultaneously finishing his assignments
2. He graded exams in the grading department of the university
3. He was appointed as an usher at the Annenberg Center
4. For the students of underprivileged background and on scholarships, he was appointed as the chemistry tutor

Doing these jobs at the university allowed him to earn around $70 dollars a week, which helped him pay for his house rent and living expenses.

Interestingly, as a tuition paying student, Penn allowed Sinha to do four courses in his semester instead of three. Apart from the mandatory courses including Math, Applied Elasticity, and a Master' thesis, he was allowed to choose an elective from any department across the university.

Alongside the compulsory subjects, Sinha took 'Introduction to Robotics' and 'Introduction to Computer Vision'. The latter was taught by a professor named Ruzena Bajcsy, whom he found very inspiring. In his mind he was certain that if he ever pursued a Ph.D., it would be under her guidance. Around the same time, he also got the opportunity to assist another Wharton Professor, Arvind Rangaswamy. The role not only gave him access to his own cabin but also offered him the chance to earn more money.

At the end of the semester, Sinha received an unexpected apology from the graduate program's head for not being able to give him a scholarship, despite his outstanding performance. A week later, a student on full scholarship withdrew from the program to move to another institute. This put Sinha on full scholarship for the rest of his tenure at Penn.

This particular turn of events cemented his confidence in his own abilities. From being unsure of his engineering aspirations, he had now succeeded academically because he was able to pursue the subjects, he was passionate about.

'Penn was truly world-class,' he recalls. ***'I saw what that meant in everyday practice—freedom for faculty, respect for research, and a sense of community that cut across departments.'***

Gaining a PhD in mechanical engineering, and simultaneously delving into the world of robotics Sinha's success in his Master's program made him realise that with enough determination and hardwork, he could succeed in anything he set his mind to. Though he was initially rejected by Professor Ruzena, his desire to do his Ph.D. under her remained unwavering. Initially, she explained to him that as someone from mechanical engineering, it didn't make sense for him to do his Ph.D. under a professor of computer science.

Upon learning that Sinha was still firm on doing his PhD under her, she revealed that there was a project with the United States Postal Service in need of a collaborator. However, she informed him that it had nothing to do with mechanical engineering and was completely computer science driven.

Observing his dedication and potential, Professor Ruzena decided to take his case to the head of the department, who eventually agreed to make an exception. As a result, Sinha earned a Ph.D. in mechanical engineering under a computer science professor—a symbolic achievement. Over the course of his research, he built up a decent academic record of publications in robotics as well, and his papers are till-date cited in scholarly research works.

THE MCKINSEY JOURNEY—FROM A PHD IN MECHANICAL ENGINEERING AND APPLIED MECHANICS TO A MANAGEMENT CONSULTANT

Dr Sinha's entry into McKinsey wasn't the outcome of a carefully planned career move. It was the result of a chance interaction with a contemporary and relative. While pursuing his Ph.D. from Penn, a family acquaintance was simultaneously enrolled in a doctoral programme at Wharton. During a coincidental meeting in Canada, she suggested applying to McKinsey. A few days later, the same advice was reinforced, with an emphasis on the firm's diversified hiring approach and its openness to candidates with unconventional academic backgrounds.

Coming from a non-traditional background for the role, applying to a globally renowned consulting firm, which predominantly hired MBA graduates from top business schools, was a bold and pivotal move. After careful consideration, he applied to the Toronto office. Despite his initial desire to move back to the US, where most of his friends and family were, his visit to the Toronto office changed everything. When he went to the office, he absolutely loved it. He was surprised to see that many people, like him, were not MBA graduates. One such example was Dominic Barton (Former Global Managing Partner at McKinsey), who was also based there at the time.

With the interview ahead, preparation became his focus. Feeling anxious yet determined, he immersed himself in reading to sharpen his business acumen, including "*The Machine that Changed the Work*" and "*The Work of Nations*". Besides, he prepared various hand-written notes to answer some of the common interview questions, a strategy he even today swears by while guiding young minds.

On the day of the interview, his extensive preparation paid off as he seamlessly displayed his quick thinking and potential to grow in a field absolutely alien to him. Coming from the mindset that advertising meant nothing but marketing, Sinha never imagined he would clear nine interviews and three rounds. But to his surprise, it all worked out and he decided to join.

On the first day, he picked up a copy of McKinsey's monthly magazine that featured brilliant Indian minds who had been hired to lead the company's recently opened branch in India. This was a powerful moment as it subtly hinted at the tremendous growth he was about to experience in India.

More than acting as a stepping stone into the corporate landscape, McKinsey allowed Sinha to immerse himself into an intense learning environment, something he had not experienced in academia. ***'My whole grounding in values, business values in particular, major commitment to people, which I learned there, shaped my professional journey.'***

The firm played a critical role in his confidence and strategic thinking. There, he was put through a four-week bootcamp called 'Mini MBA', where a few initiatives and suggestions made by him turned him into the lead faculty of that program. It was there where he was compelled to engage in client communications, conflict management, manage business complexities, and learn to lead.

Sinha also came to understand that true leadership lies in making others successful. At every step of his McKinsey journey, he was guided by his seniors and mentors who constantly pushed him to challenge his limits yet never left him feeling isolated.

Little did he know at the time that these lessons would define his future. When he transitioned to education to build new ecosystems through ISB, Ashoka University and Harappa, he carried with him and applied the coaching and lifelong learning he acquired at McKinsey.

A SURPRISING TURN—BECOMING THE 'UNPLANNED' FOUNDING DEAN OF ISB

Another institution that redefined the professional journey of Sinha was when he became the founding dean of ISB (Indian School of Business). ISB was a project initiated by a group of visionary Indian entrepreneurs who recognized the need of establishing a business school in India, one that competed with global business schools, attract top-notch faculty from across the globe, and produce leaders that could transform the future of India.

McKinsey's then global managing director, Rajat Kumar Gupta, invited Sinha to help create a new business school in India. ISB was conceived as a one-year management programme that would match global standards and address India's shortage of world-class business education. Sinha didn't have an MBA himself, something Gupta told him was an advantage. ***'Not having an MBA gives you an edge,'*** he said, ***'because you can imagine a business school differently.'***

The ISB journey, with Sinha serving as the founding Dean, gave him both confidence and a template. He saw how collective philanthropy could create a self-governing institution and how rigorous design could be a substitute for legacy.

'The success of ISB gave me the conviction that we in India could build institutions that are globally benchmarked, if we set high standards and stayed patient.'

Sinha bought with him a strategic mindset that smoothly blended corporate efficiency and academic discipline. In less than a decade, ISB, with its one-year post-graduate program format, visiting faculty model, and innovation in executive education, rose to become one of the top business schools across the globe, positioning India as a prime destination for management studies.

Stemming from his own educational journey, Sinha envisioned a school that could offer premium quality education to Indian students without requiring them to leave the country or grapple with the financial burdens of moving abroad. Interestingly, Sinha was never meant to be the founding dean, the role was supposed to be fulfilled by two others who were eventually not able to make it. When that happened, Sinha was considered the most suitable and fitting choice to execute the expected responsibilities.

Though many people including his wife were not in favour of him jeopardizing his career at McKinsey in the long run, people like Rajendra Pawar (Co-founder and Chairman of NIIT) and Donald Jacobs (Former Dean, Northwestern University of Kellogg School of Management) explained to him how it was a life changing opportunity to leave a lasting legacy in the space of education. Encouraged, he took the opportunity and changed the face of business education in India.

Today, the institution stands as an exemplar of world-class learning. At ISB, learning is deeply embedded in real-world problem solving. The school runs 163 live projects in parallel across 105 organisations, including Google and

Apollo Hospitals. These partnerships bring actual business challenges into the classroom, enabling students to build strong problem-solving capabilities and navigate complex professional environments with confidence.

Alongside this experiential learning, AI is beginning to redefine how ISB approaches teaching. Rather than replacing the classroom, AI deepens engagement before students enter it. Learners now work with AI case companions to effectively understand extensive business cases, simulate the perspective of the protagonist, and allow students to interrogate the problem in advance, helping them make informed decisions.

That said, this is just the beginning. ISB is set to keep evolving as leadership, technology, and management continue to intersect, unfolding new dimensions of growth together.

FROM CLASSROOMS TO MEDIA—BRIEF VENTURES BEFORE MOVING BACK TO ACADEMIA

After founding ISB in 2001 as its founding dean and building an institution with a lasting legacy, Sinha subsequently returned to McKinsey where he had built a strong professional reputation. Yet the experience of creating ISB left a lasting impression on his aspirations. It clarified that his interests lay beyond advisory roles, towards the deeper purpose of building institutions from the ground up.

This evolving sense of purpose led him to the ABP group (Ananda Bazar Patrika), one of India's largest media conglomerates, in 2007. As the CEO and Managing Director, he oversaw various publications and media properties, gained critical experience in managing large organizations, and gathered insights around the constantly evolving media landscape.

REIMAGINING HIGHER EDUCATION WITH THE BIRTH OF ASHOKA UNIVERSITY

After gaining years of experience in shaping institutions, Pramath set out on a journey to build something more unconventional and ground-breaking: a liberal arts university in India that met global standards. Around 2007-2008, he started engaging more with like-minded educators, entrepreneurs, and philanthropists who shared a common frustration—India's narrow education system.

Even during his days at IIT Kanpur, Sinha had realised that the Indian society was fixated on equating success with fields like engineering, business, and medical science, which often led to career switches or career dissatisfaction among many. While he was fortunate enough to find his true interests and grow under the guidance of excellent professors and mentors, a majority of Indian students blindly followed the herd. Barely anyone was eager to pursue their passions or step away from the conventionally considered ideal career paths at the time. And a few who displayed the courage to get into creative fields didn't have the right set of resources and support in the country.

The purpose to build an institution that offered interdisciplinary learning models like Ivy league schools led to the establishment of Ashoka University in 2014. Over the next few years, Sinha and his cofounders brought more than 100 founding donors under one roof, facilitating the common vision of redefining the higher education system in India. Many of these founders and professionals not only contributed financially but also offered their time, energy, and credibility in turning their shared dream into reality. ISB had taught Sinha that community, conviction, and collaboration were important pillars for building an institution.

What made Ashoka even more distinctive at a time when universities were experimenting with their education models was its shared governance model, a practice that is strictly followed even today. Pushing each contributor and founder to take turns to embrace leadership roles helped Ashoka to maintain transparency and accountability—an innovative institutional strategy.

Since its launch, Ashoka has emerged as a pioneer in offering a fresh take on learning with its curriculum that allows students to explore their interests across areas of humanities, social sciences, and impact. The Young India Fellowship program which was launched in 2011 as a one-year post graduate program served as a successful example that India was ready for such a model—one that emphasized on interdisciplinary learning and holistic growth of the students.

THE HARAPPA IMAGINATION—A DIGITAL PLATFORM FOR ADDRESSING LEARNING GAPS

While Ashoka University continues to thrive and evolve, Sinha understood that degrees alone cannot equip individuals with the skills needed for the evolving workplace needs and success.

With the idea to bridge the gaps between classroom to career, Sinha with his cofounder Shreyasi Singh, former managing editor of *Inc. India*, laid the foundation for Harappa, a digital learning platform that focussed on what they termed as "Thrive Skills", an essential set of cognitive, social, and behavioural skills that allow individuals to grow at every stage of their career. It became an intersection of technology, lifelong learning, and impact.

The programs strategically curated were delivered in formats that were best suited for working professionals; short, engaging, and outcome oriented. Whether an individual was a first-time manager or had taken on a senior role, the course ensured to unlock their potential, making their transitions seamless and impactful.

To further scale this model's growth, Sinha agreed for Upgrad's (an Indian edtech player) acquisition of Harappa for a deal of Rs 300 Crores in July 2022. Now merged into a single entity, both continue to act as a strong combined force to anchor the shared vision of creating a new wave of lifelong learners who are better equipped to navigate the workplace as well as market challenges.

Vedica Scholars Programme—Empowering Women Leaders

Much like Ashoka University and Harappa, Sinha co-founded another initiative in 2015, called Vedica Scholars

Programme for Women. Their mission has been to help high-performing women reach their full potential, find meaningful employment, navigate workplace challenges, and crack the glass ceiling. The eighteen-month long programme integrates management with liberal arts, offers faculty from globally renowned institutions like Harvard, Stanford, Yale, and McKinsey, and assists women in building on their leadership styles.

Moreover, not only each student is paired with a mentor for assistance every step of their journey but also receives internship and placement support to help them make a mark for themselves in the corporate landscape. In essence, Vedica is not just a business school for women, it's an incubator that helps them lead and thrive in a world that is struggling to overcome the obstacle of gender equality.

A BLUEPRINT THAT CONTINUES TO EXPAND—SINHA'S JOURNEY OF RELENTLESSLY BUILDING CONTINUES

Even after leaving a mark on the higher education sector of India through Ashoka University, changing the face of business management education in India through ISB, redefining professional learning through Harappa, and empowering women leadership through Vedica Scholars Programme, Pramath Sinha shows no sign of taking a back seat and retiring.

His recent venture Jetri, an evolved version of 9.9 Education, a venture started by Sinha and his co-founders a decade ago, is a testament to how he continues to bring together leaders and entrepreneurs to revolutionize the Indian education ecosystem. Partnering with schools, colleges, and universities, it supports both the creation of new institutions and the strengthening of existing ones, while also advising philanthropists and education visionaries on launching initiatives critical to India's learning ecosystem.

Its work spans institution building, programme expansion, India entry strategies for global institutions, leadership and faculty development, and the identification of world class academic talent. Distinctively, Jetri operates beyond advisory, working closely with partners on the ground to translate vision into execution and lasting institutional impact.

'My own work with ISB and Ashoka is not done; I would really like to pursue those. We have strong teams in Jetri and other initiatives that we have launched, so I would like to continue to support them in making those successful. I will be less on the hook to manage, grow, raise money, and deliver, as we have strong teams to do that. I would also like to do something for Bihar, my home state.'

At a closer look, it is evident that every venture started by Sinha is a strategic and outcome-oriented response to the problems he witnessed in the society. His journey is a reminder of how true success doesn't come from chasing glory; it comes from using your skills and potential for resolving greater problems in order to create a long-term impact.

From a young boy at IIT who wasn't confident of his own abilities to becoming a leader in the education landscape responsible for empowering thousands of individuals, his story is nothing short of inspiring. At every phase of life, what truly helped in propelling his career forward was his dedication to his dreams, seeking guidance whenever required, and viewing success not as a personal victory but rather as a significant contribution to the society.

'Education made a big difference to my life but now I have the ability to affect many lives through education.'

For him, the idea is simple: if you want to witness change, make it happen. Take the reins in your control and chart the course. Create institutions and impact that drives true change.

CHAPTER 12

The World As His Classroom

Sunny Varkey, Founder of GEMS Education

'One vision, shared learning and belonging.'

WHERE IT ALL BEGAN: A FAMILY'S MISSION TO TRANSFORM THE EDUCATION LANDSCAPE

Sunny Varkey, a visionary, now celebrated as one of the greatest entrepreneurs, reformers, and philanthropists of our time, was born in Kerala, India, in 1957. His parents, K.S. Varkey and Mariamma Varkey, were both highly dedicated teachers who instilled in him a deep respect for learning from a very young age.

'Whatever the question, education is the answer.'

But he wasn't born with a silver spoon in his mouth. At just eleven years old, he started selling fruits to support his family; a modest beginning that taught him resilience and the importance of perseverance in the face of life's challenges. It is through unwavering dedication that he has risen to a position where he impacts millions of lives each day in the most meaningful way.

In the latter half of the 1950s, the Gulf region started opening itself to expatriates for work and entrepreneurship opportunities, especially attracting interest from South-Asian communities. Recognising the growing need for expatriates to learn and excel in English-language education, K.S. Varkey took the chance and moved to Dubai in 1959, and Mariamma Varkey followed in 1961. Meanwhile, Sunny remained in the care of his grandmother in Kerala and attended a catholic boarding school in Kollam city. With limited infrastructure and resources, Mariamma Varkey began teaching children from low-income homes, slowly laying the foundation for what would eventually become an educational legacy the whole world would be astonished to discover.

In the late 1960s, Dubai was still in the early stages of development, far from the luxury malls, skyscrapers and world-class infrastructure it has today. At the time, expatriates had very limited options for their children's education, as not many had access to government-aided or public schools, and private institutions were still gaining momentum. Addressing this gap, the Varkeys opened their own school, "Our Own English High School", in 1968. Not long after, Sunny moved to Dubai to rejoin his parents.

'If you look at the name, it does not cater to any particular community. It does not have a catholic inclination or an Indianized name. Plus, the population in Dubai of Indian immigrants was small. So, my father said why don't we

call it "Our English High School", so that it can serve any nationality, and that's how we named our first school.'

Offering structured, affordable and value-based education, the school instantly became a beacon of hope for the immigrant community. Little did they know then that this trusted institution would eventually grow into a much broader vision, GEMS Education, one of the world's leading K-12 education providers.

The Varkeys established "Our Own English High School" in Bastakiya, one of the oldest and most historically significant parts of Dubai. While Sunny was studying in another part of the country, he was closely involved with the school's journey and often helped his mother with various responsibilities as it steadily grew. In 1980, he formally took over the family business, marking the beginning of its transformation into a global education enterprise.

FROM HEALTHCARE TO HOSPITALITY TO EDUCATION—HOW CROSS-INDUSTRY EXPERIENCE SHAPED A YOUNG ENTREPRENEUR'S BUSINESS ACUMEN

Sunny Varkey's business journey began long before he supported the family school, forged through hands-on experiences in the real world. His education was in a boarding school in Kerala, and he would sell fruits with his cousin to pedestrians during summer holidays.

Rather than relying on his parents for pocket money, he chose to earn it himself. Though a decent student, academics didn't really excite the young Sunny Varkey, whereas the spark of becoming an entrepreneur burned brightly, motivating him to steer his career in that direction.

Alongside supporting his mother's school, Sunny also embarked on his own business journey. But he didn't dive straight into the education sector, instead choosing to gain numerous experiences in different fields. He opened his first business in 1978, followed by a trading company in 1979, and in 1980 became a partner in a hotel. The same year, he also took over the management of his mother's school. Over time, he expanded into the healthcare industry, before completely dedicating himself to education. Across all the ventures, what remained constant was Sunny's mindset of serving people.

Each industry experience added unique value to Varkey's professional journey. While the healthcare industry taught him to empathize with both patients and doctors before forming judgments, the hotel industry demanded a cheerful and welcoming attitude, pushing him to explore and leverage his interpersonal skills. These experiences not only meticulously carved the leader in him but also allowed him to understand his own potential.

Though he operated across a range of industries, Sunny came to realise that education is the most powerful catalyst for achieving broader goals such as poverty eradication, gender equality, and improved health outcomes. A consistent theme in his speeches, especially those tied to the Varkey Foundation, has been that the global education crisis, where

272 million children around the world are still not enrolled in school, is not treated with enough urgency by policymakers.

'We must be clear that we have a global education crisis on our hands. It may not appear on the evening news or be trending on X. Perhaps that is because its impact on the individual, their family and community, is gradual rather than dramatic. It doesn't lend itself to a simple powerful photo that shows the suffering of its victims. But it is there—a cancer slowly eating away at the futures of young people around the world.'

In the 1970s, Dubai's population began to grow rapidly, and with the formation of the UAE in 1971, the nation stood at the brink of a new dawn. The gradual influx of expatriates, combined with the country's vision for development, demanded robust infrastructure, particularly in terms of services like healthcare and education. Sunny Varkey recognised this incredible opportunity to not just establish a business but to thrive alongside the country.

As Dubai evolved from a modest trading hub to a rich melting pot of cultures, the demand for quality education soared. At the same time, healthcare became a national priority, and Sunny could see how healthcare and education were intertwined with economic and social development.

'As Dubai started growing in population, and the UAE was formed, we started growing with the country. Soon education and healthcare became very important to the country.'

As a result, Varkey's journey became inseparable from the UAE's own growth story; a powerful example of how when vision, timing, and determination align, they create a lasting impact. His legacy now serves as an inspiration for other nations striving to build their futures on the foundations of education and empowerment.

HALF A MILLION ALUMNI—VARKEY'S VISION TO TURN A FAMILY SCHOOL INTO ONE OF THE WORLD'S LEADING K-12 EDUCATION PROVIDERS

After excelling in the hospitality and healthcare industries, Sunny became determined to scale the impact of the Varkey family school. He saw education as the most powerful way to impact people and decided to move beyond the single-school model, opening diverse institutions to meet the varied needs of families.

This led to the birth of GEMS (Global Management Education Systems)—a company built on the idea that education should be inclusive, flexible, and globally relevant. Crucially, Sunny pioneered high-quality education across curricula, cultures, and socio-economic backgrounds. From British and Indian curricula to American, IB, and other education systems, GEMS started curating programmes well-tailored to international and local communities, ensuring every student could find a suitable learning environment.

This inclusive approach allowed GEMS to rapidly grow. Back then, their family school charged a modest fee of 90-100 dirhams. Today, with a team of exceptional people operating in multiple regions, GEMS Education charges annual fees ranging from around US $1,000 to US $40,000 per annum, depending on the school and curriculum.

GEMS Education is now one of the world's leading private K-12 education providers, educating more than 200,000 students from 176+ nationalities across its global network of owned and managed schools. With nearly half a million alumni, GEMS has built a legacy of impact that spans generations and continents. Additionally, to ensure that each student receives excellent support from teachers, GEMS employs thousands of teachers globally, making it one of the largest employers of educators.

Now, drawing on more than sixty-five years of experience, running successful schools across multiple curricula, Varkey has launched GEMS School Management (GSM) to partner with investors, developers and governments to open new schools, and work with existing school owners to raise academic results, grow enrolment and positively impact their communities.

However, reflecting on his expansion strategy, Sunny admits to making some mistakes. When GEMS expanded out of the UAE, to countries where the brand wasn't known, it initially struggled with a few challenges like mapping out strategies that could have been implemented differently. But an excellent visionary is one who knows exactly when and how to pivot. Today, GEMS continues to expand its wings to ensure children are empowered through education.

Sunny has always believed that the most important gift a parent can give their child is a strong education and the values that shape their character. Beyond delivering academic excellence, GEMS is renowned for building a deep sense of community, helping young people flourish in a rapidly globalised world.

It is why Mr Varkey is so passionate about the importance of family, recently launching his Family First initiative, a transformative movement that seeks to empower global change through love, care, and shared stories, with a focus on strengthening family and community bonds across generations. It actively seeks to foster intergenerational learning, and combat issues such as loneliness, isolation, and depression.

'Families that stand together, united, are always stronger. And for those that say our elders are merely dependents, I say this to you ... Have you ever seen grandparents play with their grandchildren? You will see that our elders are the essential anchors of stability and guidance. They offer deep wisdom, important traditions, and a huge capacity for love.'

VARKEY FOUNDATION—EMBRACING PHILANTHROPY

'I was fortunate that I grew up in a family where charity was ingrained in us from a very early age. Even when my father earned a small amount, a large portion was shared with the community we lived in, sometimes at the cost of

our own comfort. To this day, our underlying philosophy remains that good giving pinches, meaning that the sacrifice you make has to be felt. Therein lies the appeal of the Giving Pledge to my family.'

In 2015, Mr Varkey became the first education entrepreneur to sign the Giving Pledge. The Varkey Foundation, his family foundation launched in 2010, focuses on influencing global education policy and advocating for the status of teachers.

Soon after launching the Varkey Foundation, Sunny and his team reflected on what more could be done for teachers. To gain a better understanding of how the teaching profession is perceived in different countries, the foundation conducted the world's first Global Teacher Status Index. The Varkey family were shocked to find that teachers weren't receiving the respect or recognition they deserved around the world.

With this in mind, the Global Teacher Prize, often referred to as the "Nobel Prize for Teaching", was launched in 2014. The prize, which now partners with UNESCO, awards US $1 million to one exceptional teacher who has made an outstanding contribution to the profession. It was set up to shine a spotlight on the important role teachers play in society and since 2014 has unearthed thousands of inspiring stories of teachers who are transforming the lives of children around the world. The Global Teacher Prize has also inspired over forty National Teacher Prizes, becoming a beacon for teachers everywhere as well as the foundation's guiding light.

The 2020 winner was Indian village teacher Ranjitsinh Disale, selected from over 12,000 nominations and applications from over 140 countries, due to his work in transforming the life chances of young girls at the Zilla Parishad Primary School in Maharashtra.

Just this year, the Varkey Foundation also launched the US $1 million Global Schools Prize, a new award organised in collaboration with UNESCO, to honour schools re-imagining education for the future.

The Global Schools Prize joins the Global Teacher Prize and Global Student Prize, which Sunny Varkey also founded, completing a powerful trilogy that celebrates educators, learners, and now schools as institutions of innovation and change. Together, Sunny hopes the three prizes will spark a 360-degree conversation about what it takes to deliver the best possible education, equipping children to face the future with confidence, while rethinking the future of learning for generations to come.

'The Global Schools Prize is more than an award—it's a movement to reimagine learning in a world of constant change. By recognising multiple winners, we shine a light on the many ways schools are driving progress—from innovation and teacher development to sustainability and student wellbeing.'

THE NEXT FRONTIER—RE-IMAGINING EDUCATION FOR A NEW GENERATION

2025 has been a transformative year for GEMS Education. Sunny Varkey launched the GEMS School of Research and Innovation in Dubai Sports City, labelled the "finest school in the world" and designed to be a global benchmark for future-focused education, blending an enhanced English curriculum with cutting-edge AI integration, values-driven leadership, and world-class facilities.

Building on this, Varkey also launched Parent360, a programme that helps parents truly understand their children, not just their test scores, but the innate, God-given gifts that lie within. Through GEMS' Determined Genius programme, those strengths are transformed into daily habits, instilling hard work, discipline, and purpose. With Beyond100, GEMS goes even further, teaching pupils practical healthy habits that maximise the benefits of modern medical advances, empowering them to enjoy longer, happier lives.

GEMS is also nurturing students' passions and talents through dedicated academies in music, theatre, fashion, fine arts, entrepreneurship, e-sports, and even aviation.

While GEMS continues to be one of the most successful learning institutions across the globe, its core mission goes beyond scaling, rankings, and accolades. It wants to instil a strong value system in each child, so that they can all grow into responsible global citizens.

'I'm no way near perfect but I'm a very strong believer in fate. I pray every day and my success has been because of my hard work and God's continued blessings.'

It is no surprise that over his career Sunny Varkey has amassed many accolades. UNESCO, seeing the success of his work on teacher statuses, asked Sunny Varkey to become a Goodwill Ambassador, and Harvard University appointed him to their Global Advisory Council. The Indian Government also honoured Sunny Varkey with the Padma Shri award, one of India's highest civilian honours.

But despite these accolades, Sunny believes everything ultimately comes down to a simple promise.

'Our work is a simple promise which we must keep. A promise that my late mother and father made when they built that very first classroom. To always put children first. We are committed to helping them shine and succeed. It is truly an honour. Because education is not just the greatest gift you can give. It is the gift that keeps on giving, Generation after generation after generation.'

A Tapestry of Voices

When one listens carefully to the voices of those who have built, led, and reimagined education in India and beyond, what emerges is not a single melody but a rich tapestry of threads woven from childhood memories of abundance, the centrality of teachers, the necessity of scale, the quiet power of institutions, and the faith that education is both service and destiny.

Across these conversations—with **Kiran Bir Sethi, Ashish Dhawan, Shaheen Mistri, Ashwin Damera, Rajendar Pawar, Anita Karwal, Ronnie Screwvala, Prajodh Rajan, Grace Pinto, Sunny Varkey, Pramath Raj Sinha, and Dr J.C. Chaudhary**, the diversity of experience is breathtaking. Yet the lessons point to a shared truth: education is not simply the transfer of knowledge but the building block of a great society.

This closing chapter is not an end but an invitation, to carry forward the abundance of childhood, to honour teachers, to build institutions, to scale with courage, to bridge policy and practice, and to treat education as faith.

In these lessons lies the blueprint for the future.

Acknowledgements

This book would not have been possible without the generosity, time, and honesty of the remarkable leaders whose journeys we have had the privilege to document. Each of them opened their doors, their memories, and their minds to us, with candour that went far beyond interviews. Their stories, struggles, and reflections form the heart of this book, and we are deeply grateful to them for trusting us with their narratives.

We extend our heartfelt gratitude to Ashish Dhawan, JC Chaudhry, Shaheen Mistri, Kiranbir Sethi, Grace Pinto, Pramath Raj Sinha, Ashwin Damera, Anita Karwal, Sunny Varkey, Rajendra Pawar, Prajodh Rajan, and Ronnie Screwvala—leaders whose lives and work continue to shape the future of education in India. Their commitments to excellence, access, purpose, and innovation are the reason this book exists.

A special thanks to their teams and institutions, who supported our research, facilitated conversations, and helped us navigate archives, timelines, and personal histories with immense patience. We are deeply grateful to the editorial and publishing teams at HarperCollins, whose guidance, feedback, and belief in the vision of this book strengthened it at every stage. Their commitment to bringing meaningful stories to the world has been invaluable.

To the educators, administrators, parents, and students we interacted with along the way, thank you for reminding us that the impact of great leadership is most visible in everyday lives, often far away from the spotlight. To our own families and colleagues, who stood by us through long interviews, countless drafts, and months of research, your encouragement and faith kept us anchored and motivated throughout this journey.

Finally, this book is dedicated to everyone who believes that education can transform destinies. We hope these stories inspire future leaders, spark new conversations, and deepen our collective commitment to building an India where every learner can thrive.

Bibliography

1. Interviews conducted by authors

The core insights of this book have been drawn from the in-depth interviews conducted with leaders in the education, entrepreneurship, and social innovation landscape. These include:

1. Kiranbir Sethi—Founder, Riverside School and Design initiative
2. Grace and Ryan Pinto—Founder and CEO, Ryan International Group
3. Prajodh Rajan—Co-Founder & Group CEO, Lighthouse Learning
4. Ronnie Screwvala—Chairperson & Co-Founder, Upgrad
5. Shaheen Mistri—Founder, Akanksha Foundation and Teach for India
6. Ashwin Damera—Founder and CEO, Eruditus and Emeritu
7. Rajendar Singh Pawar—Founder and Chairman, NIIT

8. Dr J.C. Chaudhry—Founder and Chairman, Aakash Educational Services
9. Ashish Dhawan—Founder, ChrysCapital; Founder, Central Square Foundation; Founder and CEO, The Convergence Foundation; and Founding Chairperson, Ashoka University
10. Anita Karwal—Former IAS Officer; Former Secretary, Department of school Education, Ministry of Education
11. Pramath Raj Sinha—Founding Dean, Indian School of Business (ISB); Founder & Trustee, Ashoka University; Founder & Chairman, Harappa Education.
12. Sunny Varkey—Founder, GEMS Education Group and Varkey Foundation

2. Conversations (YouTube Podcasts and Talks)

1. Pawar, Rajendar. Conversation titled "The Untold NIIT Story" on *The Founder Thesis Podcast*, hosted by Akshay Datt, YouTube, 2023.
2. Pawar, Rajendar. Conversation at EdTech Founders Growthcamp, YouTube, 2023.
3. Dhawan, Ashish. Conversation titled "From $4 Billion Fund Manager to Nation Builder: The Ashish Dhawan Story" on *Create Wealth with Sandeep Jethwani,* hosted by Sandeep Jethwani, YouTube, 2025.

4. Dhawan, Ashish. Conversation titled "Building Ashoka University, Advising Bill Gates, Driving India's Growth" on Sushasan, The Podcast, hosted by Guarav Goel, YouTube, 2023.
5. Dhawan, Ashish. Conversation titled "Ei Dialogues with Ashish Dhawan", on Ei_Study Podcast, hosted by Pranav Kothari, YouTube, 2020.
6. Sinha, Pramath Raj. Conversation titled "Founding ISB & Ashoka, Working with Governments across the World and the Problem with IITs", on The Barber Shop with Shantanu Podcast, hosted by Shantanu Deshpande, YouTube, 2023.

3. Books

Sethi, Kiran Bir, *EVERY CHILD CAN,* HarperCollins, 2024.

Other References

https://www.nga.gov/features/slideshows/patrons-and-artists-in-late-15th-century-florence.html

https://www.milanartinstitute.com/blog/art-lessons-from-da-vinci

http://www.italianrenaissanceresources.com/units/unit-3/essays/training-and-practice/

https://www.dataforindia.com/enrolment-in-education/

https://scholar.harvard.edu/sites/scholar.harvard.edu/files/goldin/files/_goldinkerrolivetti_ifs.pd

About the Authors

Rakesh Gupta is the Founder and Managing Partner of LoEstro Advisors, India's #1 ranked advisory firm in the education sector. Rakesh brings over fifteen years of experience in fundraise, M&A and strategy, and has experience of closing transactions exceeding $2Bn and advising leading education groups of the country. Rakesh graduated from ISB and IIT Kharagpur, is an Ex-McKinsey strategy consultant and Ex-Microsoft SDE, and has co-authored two books on education, "*Don't Build Your School Brand Without Us*" and "*Don't Build Your University Brand Without Us*". Rakesh is an alumnus of IIT Kharagpur and ISB Hyderabad.

Udayan Nath works with the education and emerging clients practice at LoEstro Advisors, one of India's fastest growing investment banking firms, and covers businesses across education, consumer, technology and allied sectors for M&A and equity fundraising mandates. Udayan carries over three years of work experience and is a LinkedIn Top Voice with 30K+ community. Udayan is a graduate from Christ University, Bangalore.

Sumit Handa is a seasoned business leader, advisor, and entrepreneur with over two decades of deep experience in advising 100+ leading education ventures of the country across various areas of strategy, marketing and operations. Sumit brings deep operating experience at one of India's leading international K-12 groups, and FMCG giants including Tata Consumer Products and ITC. Sumit graduated from SCMHRD and has co-authored two books on education, "*Don't Build Your School Brand Without Us*" and "*Don't Build Your University Brand Without Us*".

HarperCollins *Publishers* India

At HarperCollins India, we believe in telling the best stories and finding the widest readership for our books in every format possible. We started publishing in 1992; a great deal has changed since then, but what has remained constant is the passion with which our authors write their books, the love with which readers receive them, and the sheer joy and excitement that we as publishers feel in being a part of the publishing process.

Over the years, we've had the pleasure of publishing some of the finest writing from the subcontinent and around the world, including several award-winning titles and some of the biggest bestsellers in India's publishing history. But nothing has meant more to us than the fact that millions of people have read the books we published, and that somewhere, a book of ours might have made a difference.

As we look to the future, we go back to that one word—a word which has been a driving force for us all these years.

Read.

Harper Collins · Harper Sport · HARPER FICTION · HARPER NON-FICTION · हार्पर हिन्दी

HARPER LEARNING · HARPER VANTAGE · HCCB HARPERCOLLINS CHILDREN'S BOOKS · 4th · HARPER PERENNIAL

HARPER DESIGN · BOOKTOPUS · HARPER BUSINESS